DORLING KINDERSLEY 📖 EYEWITNESS BOOKS

INSECT

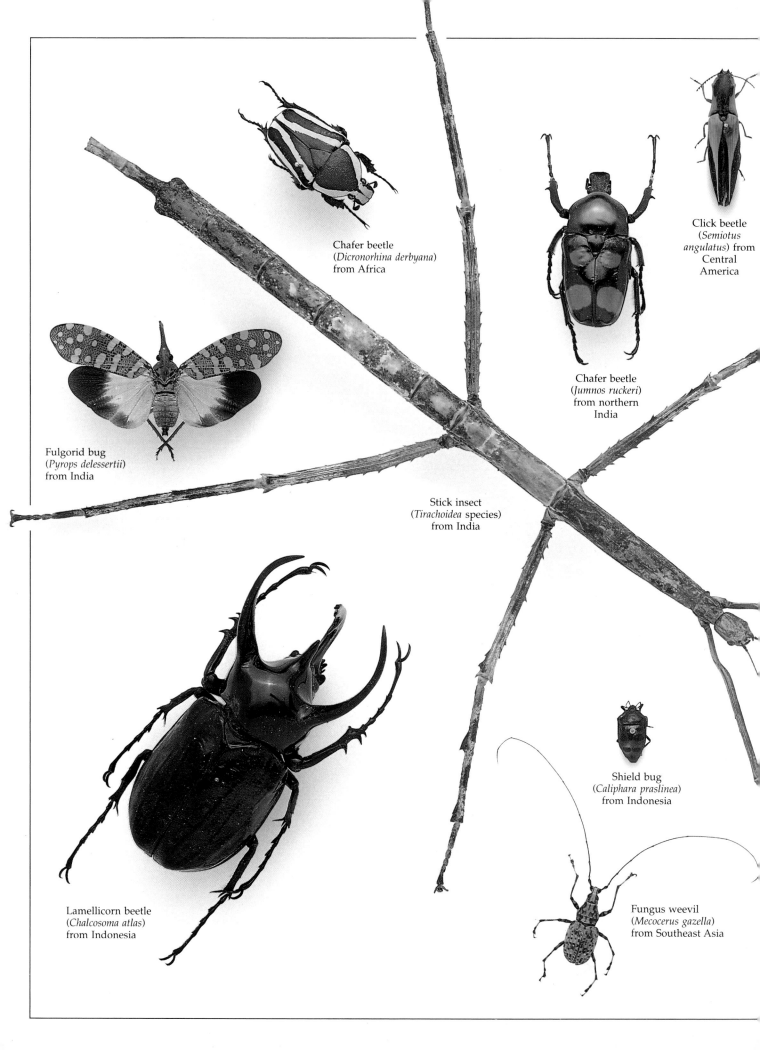

Chafer beetle
(*Dicronorhina derbyana*)
from Africa

Click beetle
(*Semiotus
angulatus*) from
Central
America

Chafer beetle
(*Jumnos ruckeri*)
from northern
India

Fulgorid bug
(*Pyrops delessertii*)
from India

Stick insect
(*Tirachoidea* species)
from India

Shield bug
(*Caliphara praslinea*)
from Indonesia

Lamellicorn beetle
(*Chalcosoma atlas*)
from Indonesia

Fungus weevil
(*Mecocerus gazella*)
from Southeast Asia

Blowfly (*Calliphora vomitoria*) found worldwide

Tawny mining bee (*Andrena fulva*) from Europe

DK EYEWITNESS BOOKS

INSECT

Stag beetle (*Phalacrognathus mulleri*) from northern Australia

Written by
LAURENCE MOUND

Bog bush cricket (*Metrioptera brachyptera*) from Europe

Leaf beetle (*Doryphorella 22-punctata*) from South America

Tortoise beetle (*Eugenysa regalis*) from South America

Shield bug (*Sphaerocoris annulus*) from Africa

Cuckoo wasp (*Stilbum splendidum*) from Australia

Longhorn beetle (*Callipogon senex*) from Central America

Rove beetle (*Emus hirtus*) from Great Britain

Shield bug (*Cantao ocellatus*) from Indonesia

Dorling Kindersley

Leaf beetle (*Doryphorella princeps*) from South America

Butterfly (*Ancycluris formosissima*) from South America

Shield bug (*Poecilocoris latus*) from India

Bilberry bumblebee (*Bombus monticola*) from Europe

Dung beetle (*Phanaeus demon*) from Central America

Dung beetle (*Coprophanaeus lancifer*) from South America

DK

Dorling Kindersley
LONDON, NEW YORK, AUCKLAND, DELHI, JOHANNESBURG, MUNICH, PARIS and SYDNEY

For a full catalog, visit

DK www.dk.com

Project editor Helen Parker
Art editor Peter Bailey
Senior editor Sophie Mitchell
Senior art editor Julia Harris
Editorial director Sue Unstead
Art director Anne-Marie Bulat
Special photography
Colin Keates, Neil Fletcher, Frank Greenaway, Jane Burton,
Kim Taylor, and Oxford Scientific Films

This Eyewitness ® Book has been conceived by
Dorling Kindersley Limited and Editions Gallimard

© 1990 Dorling Kindersley Limited
This edition © 2000 Dorling Kindersley Limited
First American edition, 1990

Published in the United States by
Dorling Kindersley Publishing, Inc.
375 Hudson Street,
New York, New York 10014

6 8 10 9 7 5

Dorling Kindersley books are available at special discounts for bulk
purchases for sales promotions or premiums. Special editions, including
personalized covers, excerpts of existing guides, and corporate imprints
can be created in large quantities for specific needs. For more information,
contact Special Markets Dept., Dorling Kindersley Publishing, Inc.,
95 Madison Ave., New York, NY 10016; Fax: (800) 600-9098

Library of Congress Cataloging-in-Publication Data
Mound, L. A. (Laurence Alfred)
Insect / written by Laurence Mound;
photographed by Colin Keates, Neil Fletcher
and Frank Greenaway.
p. cm. — (Eyewitness Books)
Includes index.
Summary: a photo essay about insects and their crucial role
in the lives of other living things.
1. Insects — Juvenile literature. [1. Insects.] I. Title.
QL467.2.M68   2000   595.7—dc20 89-15603
ISBN 0-7894-5817-9 (pb)
ISBN 0-7894-5816-0 (hc)

Color reproduction by Colourscan, Singapore
Printed in China by Toppan Printing Co. (Shenzhen) Ltd.

Tree wasp (*Dolichovespula sylvestris*) from Europe

Jewel beetle (*Chrysochroa chinensis*) from India

Giant ant (*Dinoponera grandis*) from Brazil

Chafer beetle (*Agestrata luzonica*) from the Philippines

Longhorn beetle (*Sternotomis bohemanni*) from East Africa

Tiger beetle (*Mantichora scabra*) from East Africa

Dusky sallow moth (*Eremobia ochroleuca*) from Europe

Chafer (*Trichaulax macleayi*) from northern Australia

Contents

Lamellicorn larva
(*Oryctes centaurus*)
from New Guinea

The parts of an insect

An adult insect never grows any larger. It cannot, because it has a hard, external skeleton composed largely of a tough, horny substance called chitin. This "exoskeleton" covers all parts of the body, including the legs, feet, eyes, antennae, and even the internal breathing tubes, or tracheae. Young insects must molt, or shed all these surfaces, several times during their lives in order to grow to adult size. Beneath the old, hard skin, a new, soft skeleton forms. The insect takes in extra air to make itself larger and splits the old skin, which falls off. The young stages of many insects are grubs or caterpillars (pp. 24–25), which are very different from the adults; but these also molt, eventually producing a pupa or a chrysalis.

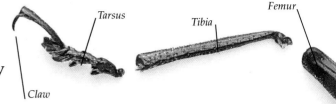

Tarsus

Tibia

Femur

Claw

Folding point

Front, or leading edge, of wing

Tip, or apex, of wing

Base of wing folds underneath

HIND WING FOLDED
In order to fit beneath the wing cases, the larger hind wings, with which the beetle flies (pp. 12–13), must be folded. The wing tip, or apex, is folded back at a special break known as the folding point in the front, or leading edge. The base of the wing is also folded underneath.

BEETLE BODY
This adult jewel beetle (*Euchroma gigantea*), shown here at three times life size, comes from South America. It is a typical insect with three distinct body regions – the head, thorax, and abdomen. As in other arthropods (pp. 8–9), these regions are all made up of small ringlike segments, and the legs are jointed.

ABDOMEN
The abdomen of an insect contains most of its "maintenance equipment" – the digestive system, heart, and sexual organs. Like the other parts of the body it is protected by the rigid exoskeleton, or cuticle, which is composed mainly of horny chitin. But between the segments the body is flexible. The whole surface is covered by a thin layer of wax which keeps the insect from losing too much water.

Ganglion in head (brain)

Nervous system

Compound eye

Foregut breaks up food

INTERNAL ANATOMY
This illustration shows the internal anatomy of a worker bee. Along the center of its body is the digestive system (yellow), which is a continuous tube divided into the foregut, midgut, and hindgut. The breathing, or respiratory, system (white) consists of a network of branched tubes, through which air passes from the spiracles to every part of the body. The two large air sacs in the abdomen are important for supplying the flight muscles in the thorax with air. The bee's heart is a long, thin tube, which pumps blood along most of the upper part of the body. There are no other blood vessels. Blood leaves the heart to carry food to the other organs. The simple nervous system (blue) is formed by one main nerve, which has knots of massed nerve cells, or ganglia, along its length. The ganglion in the head is the insect's brain. The female sexual organs and store of poison leading to the sting are shown in green.

Air sacs are important in supplying muscles in thorax with enough air for flight

Midgut digests food

Excess water is removed from the remains of food in the hindgut

Air enters breathing tubes through spiracles

Sting

Food waste is ejected through anus

Poison store for sting

FRONT WING
In beetles (pp. 30–31) the front pair of wings is adapted as a pair of hard wing cases called elytra. These protect the body and are often brightly colored. When the beetle flies (pp. 12–13), the elytra are held forward.

LEGS

Insects have three pairs of jointed legs (pp. 18–19), which are used for walking, running, or jumping – depending on the species. Each leg has four main parts: the coxa joins the leg to the thorax; the femur, or thigh, is the most muscular section of the leg; the tibia, or lower leg, often carries a number of spines for self-defense; and the tarsus, the equivalent of a human foot, consists of between one and five segments, also two claws between which there is sometimes a small pad for gripping smooth surfaces.

Tarsus has between one and five segments

Tibia

Femur

Coxa

Coxa

Second and third segments of the thorax each bear a pair of wings and a pair of legs

ARMOR PLATING

A tank is like a large beetle, with its hard outer skin protecting the important inner workings from being damaged by enemies.

Each foot bears two claws for climbing on rough surfaces

FEEDING IN INFORMATION

The head carries the feeding apparatus (pp. 20–21) as well as important sense organs such as the compound eyes (pp. 14–15), antennae (pp. 16–17), and the palps, or feelers, which are attached to the mouthparts and help give the insect information about the taste and smell of its food.

Compound eye

ANTENNAE

The antennae of insects (pp. 16–17) vary in size and shape from long and thin, as in crickets, to short and hairlike, as in some flies. Whatever their shape, the antennae bear many sensory structures that are able to detect air movements, vibrations, and smells.

COMPOUND EYES

Insect eyes (pp. 14–15) are called "compound" because each is made up of hundreds of tiny, simple eyes. These eyes enable an insect to detect movement around it in almost every direction at once.

First segment of thorax bears front pair of legs

Segmented antenna detects vibrations and smells

THORAX

The thorax is made up of three segments. The first bears the first pair of legs and is often clearly separated from the second and third segments, each of which has a pair of wings and a pair of legs. The second and third segments are closely joined to the abdomen.

Claw

Leading edge of hind wing

A spiracle can be closed to prevent the entry of air and control water loss

HIND WING OUTSTRETCHED

The wings have no muscles in them. As the wing cases are lifted, muscles inside the thorax pull on the leading edge of the hind wings and make them open automatically (pp. 12–13).

Wing case, or elytron

A BREATH OF FRESH AIR

Insects breathe air through a network of tubes (tracheae) that extend into the body from pairs of openings in the cuticle called spiracles. Some insects, like this caterpillar, have a pair of spiracles on each segment. More active insects often have fewer spiracles, as they can force air out of the tracheae.

What is an insect?

INSECTS ARE THE MOST SUCCESSFUL creatures in the whole of the animal kingdom. They are remarkably adaptable and live everywhere on land, in the air, and in water. Thus insects can be found in scorching deserts and in hot springs, on snowy mountain peaks and in icy lakes. Their small size means they can fit into very small places and do not need much food to live. Insects are invertebrates, meaning that, unlike mammals, fish, reptiles, and birds, they have no backbone. Insects belong to the group of invertebrates called arthropods; that is, they have a hard, protective exoskeleton (pp. 6–7) and jointed legs. However, insects are different from other arthropods because they have only six legs. Most insects also have wings, which enable them to escape from danger and to search for food over a wide area. Today there are over a million known species of insect with many more waiting to be discovered. Each species is a member of a larger group, or order, made up of other insects with the same physical features.

Ground beetle

Ladybird beetle

BEETLES
Beetles (pp. 30–31) belong to the order Coleoptera, meaning "sheath wings." The front pair of wings are hard, sheathlike coverings (elytra) that meet in the middle and protect the delicate hind wings and body.

Mayfly adult

MAYFLIES
These insects belong to the order Ephemeroptera, referring to the short lives of the adults. Young mayflies live and feed underwater.

Fly

FLIES
Flies (pp. 32–33) belong to the order Diptera, meaning "two wings," so named because, unlike other insects, flies only have one pair of wings. The hind wings are modified into tiny balancing organs, called halteres (p. 12).

Front wings are larger than hind wings

Wasp

Bee

Ant

WASPS, ANTS, AND BEES
The name of the order that includes all wasps, bees, and ants (pp. 38–39) is Hymenoptera. This means "membrane wings" and refers to their two pairs of thin, veined wings. The males of this order are unusual because they develop from unfertilized eggs. Many females in this group are armed with a sting.

COCKROACHES
These flattened insects (p. 41) have hardened front wings that overlap each other. Young cockroaches look like smaller versions of the adults but without wings.

Piercing, sucking mouthparts

Wings hard at base, soft at tip

Bug

Stick insect

BUGS
The name of the order of true bugs (pp. 36–37), Hemiptera, means "half wing" and refers to the front wings of many larger bugs, which are hard at the base but soft at the tip. Bugs have jointed piercing and sucking mouthparts.

Dragonfly

Earwig

DRAGONFLIES AND DAMSELFLIES
These two insects (p. 41) are closely related and belong to the order Odonata. The name refers to their large, specially adapted jaws which they use to catch flies. The nymphs live underwater and only come to the surface when it is time for the adult to emerge (pp. 26–27).

EARWIGS
The order to which earwigs (p. 41) belong is Dermaptera, meaning "skin wings." This refers to the hind wings, which are kept curiously folded under very short front wings.

Folded wings

Butterfly

Grasshopper

Moth

BUTTERFLIES AND MOTHS
These insects (pp. 34–35) belong to the order Lepidoptera, meaning "scale wings." This refers to the tiny scales (p. 13) that cover their bodies and wings and give them their beautiful rainbow-like colors.

CRICKETS AND GRASSHOPPERS
These insects (p. 40) belong to the order Orthoptera, meaning "straight wings." They have strong hind legs, which they use for jumping and singing.

STICK INSECTS
When resting, these long and slender insects (p. 40) look just like the twigs and leaves that they eat (p. 45).

These are not insects

Many people confuse other arthropods with insects. Spiders and scorpions not only have four pairs of legs, rather than three as insects do, but their head and thorax (pp. 6–7) are fused together in a single structure. Unlike insects they have no wings, no antennae, and small, simple eyes instead of a pair of large compound eyes (pp. 14–15). Crabs and prawns, wood lice and centipedes, all have many more jointed legs than insects – millipedes even have two pairs on each segment. In contrast an earthworm, although composed of many segments, has no legs at all, and the body does not have a distinct head. The structure of slugs, snails, and starfish is very different and is not based on segments.

VERTEBRATES
This monkey is a vertebrate, meaning it has a backbone. Birds, fish, lizards (reptiles), frogs (amphibians), and mammals are all vertebrates. They breathe with lungs or gills, and have a central heart. None of them has six legs, and their bodies are not divided into segments.

Scorpion

Pedipalps are specially adapted to form pincers

SCORPIONS
Like all arachnids, including spiders and ticks, scorpions have four pairs of legs. This scorpion from North Africa catches its prey with its big pincers, which are really a specially adapted pair of limbs, called pedipalps.

Prawn

PRAWNS
These sea-dwelling creatures have an external skeleton and ten jointed legs – eight legs for walking and two for feeding and defense.

Earthworm

EARTHWORMS
All earthworms are made up of many ringlike segments. Unlike insects they have no legs and no hard parts and it is often difficult to tell which end the head is at. Giant earthworms may be more than 6 ft (2 m) long.

Head

Ringlike segments

Millipede

Each segment bears four legs

MILLIPEDES
It is easy to see a millipede's head because, like insects, it has a pair of antennae. Unlike an insect, its body is not divided into three separate parts (pp. 6–7) but into many segments, each of which bears two pairs of legs. Millipedes often feed on plants and may be garden pests.

Wood louse

WOOD LICE
Wood lice, or pill bugs, are related to the beach flea. They need water and live in cool, damp places, under stones and logs, where they feed on rotting wood and leaves. When danger threatens they roll into a tight round ball of scaly armor.

BEACH FLEAS
These strange creatures are similar to insects in appearance, but they have ten legs, rather than an insect's six. They live in damp sand on beaches all over the world. When disturbed, they use their front two pairs of legs to jump surprising distances.

Antenna

CENTIPEDES
Unlike millipedes, with which they are often confused, centipedes have only one pair of legs on each segment. They spend their lives in the soil, feeding on other small soil-dwelling animals. Centipedes capture their prey with their "poison claws," a specially adapted front pair of legs with fangs. Large species can give a painful bite.

"Poison claws" – modified front legs – are used to catch prey

Centipede

Pedipalps used as feelers

Jaws

Leg

SPIDERS
This tarantula from Sri Lanka is one of the world's largest spiders. In front of the eight legs there is a pair of leglike appendages called pedipalps, which are used as feelers. The large jaws inject poison into the prey and, as with all spiders, the food is sucked into the body as a liquid. The large abdomen has two pairs of book lungs, like fish gills, which must be kept moist to absorb air.

Tarantula

9

The first insects

INSECT JEWELRY
Amber has been looked on as a precious stone for centuries. This piece of Baltic amber, cut and polished as a pendant, contains three very different types of flies.

THE FIRST WINGED INSECTS flew through the coal forests that covered the Earth over 300 million years ago. Early fossil remains show that a few of these insects, such as dragonflies and cockroaches (pp. 40–41), would have looked very similar to present-day species. But most of the oldest insect fossils represent groups that are no longer alive today. Some of these early insects were probably slowed down by large, unfolding wings, with spans of up to 30 in (76 cm), which prevented them from making a quick escape and made them sitting targets for hungry predators. Looking at fossils is our only means of understanding the evolution of insects, but because insects are usually small and delicate, most of them probably rotted away before they could become trapped in muddy sediments and fossilized. And so, with very little fossil evidence on which to base our conclusions, no one is yet sure how insects evolved.

Limestone fossil of a moth's wing from southern England

SHOW YOUR COLORS
Pigments in the scales of this fossilized wing have altered the process of fossilization, so that parts of the color pattern can still be seen 400 million years later.

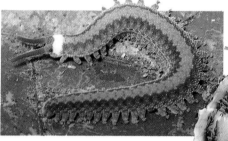

LIVING ANCESTORS?
The peripatus possibly represents a halfway stage between worms and insects. Like a worm, it has a soft body with ring-like segments. However, it has clawed legs like an insect and a similar circulatory and breathing system.

SPRINGTAILS
The primitive wingless springtails live in damp places all over the world. Many have a curious forked jumping organ folded up under their tail – hence the name. This species, shown here on the underside of a dead limpet, lives on the seashore, feeding on bacteria.

How amber is formed

Amber is the fossil resin of pine trees that flourished on Earth over 40 million years ago. As the resin oozed from cracks and wounds in the tree trunks insects attracted by the sweet scent became trapped on its sticky surface. In time the resin, including the trapped insects, hardened and was buried in the soil. Millions of years later it was then washed into the sea. Copal looks similar to amber but is much younger.

Modern-day "sweat bee" (*Trigona* species)

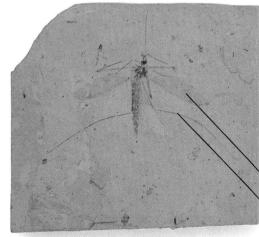

Wing

Delicate legs

EARLY CRANES
About 35 million years ago in what is now Colorado, this crane fly became trapped in muddy sediment at the bottom of a lake or a pond. The sediment was so fine that when it turned to stone, even details of the wings and legs were preserved. This fossilized specimen looks very similar to modern crane flies. The weak, drifting flight and the long, floppy legs were clearly important adaptations to life long before the American continent took its present shape.

BEE IN COPAL
This piece of copal from Zanzibar (an island off the east coast of Africa) could be 1,000 or one million years old. It has been magnified to show the beautifully preserved "sweat bee" (*Trigona* species). The bee is similar to the present-day specimen shown above.

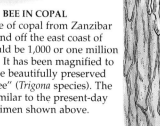

A STICKY END
Crawling and flying insects, attracted by the pine resin oozing from this tree trunk, are trapped forever. Scenes like this took place over 40 million years ago.

OLDEST DRAGONFLY

This fossilized folded wing is the oldest known dragonfly. It was found above a coal seam at Bolsover Colliery in Derbyshire, England, 2,300 ft (700 m) underground. The dragonfly flew 300 million years ago and had a total wingspan of 8 in (20 cm), considerably larger than the largest present-day species shown here.

Broken wing

FLOWERING PLANTS

The appearance of the first flowering plants about 100 million years ago signified a new source of food in the form of pollen and nectar. Insects thrived because of this new food, and the flowering plants thrived because of the variety of pollinating insects. The number of insects and plants increased together, a process known as coevolution (pp. 42–43).

LARGEST DRAGONFLY

This dragonfly (*Tetracanthagyna plagiata*) from Borneo is a member of the largest dragonfly species still in existence today. The largest dragonfly ever known is a fossilized specimen from the U.S., with a wingspan of about 24 in (60 cm).

Compound eye

Black spot, or stigma

Veins

Abdomen

Unlike the wings of more recently developed insects, dragonfly wings do not fold

DRAGONFLY PREDATORS

The artist of this whimsical engraving clearly had more imagination than biological knowledge. Present-day dragonflies are fast and skilled fliers. Fossils prove their ancestors were similar and would not have made easy prey for a pterosaur.

Tip of abdomen

Veins on wings

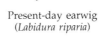

DROWNED EARWIG

The lake deposits at Florissant, Colorado, are about 35 million years old. They contain many well-preserved insect fossils because of the fine sediment from which the rocks were formed. Many of these insects would not have lived in the lake – they simply fell in and were drowned.

Present-day earwig
(*Labidura riparia*)

TURNED TO STONE

Fossilized specimens of smaller dragonfly species, such as this one from southern England, are relatively common. Even though this specimen appears to be missing a wing, it is possible to see all the veins quite clearly.

Wings and flight

Fringed veins

CRUMPLED WINGS
The wings of an adult cicada are much larger than the body (p. 36). But a newly emerged adult has small, soft crumpled wings. Blood is pumped into veins in the wings making them expand rapidly. As the veins harden, the wings straighten ready for flight.

Insects were the first creatures to fly. Flight enabled them to escape more easily from predators, and to fly to new areas in search of better food. Later, wings became important for finding and attracting a mate – by being brightly colored or by producing a scent or making sounds. But the origin of wings is not understood. Some early wingless insects may initially have gained an advantage over others by gliding from trees using pairs of primitive flaps on several segments of their body. Gradually, because two pairs of flaps are more efficient in the air, wings evolved.

The earliest known flying insects, like dragonflies today, had two pairs of independently flapping wings that did not fold. More recent insects, such as butterflies, wasps, and beetles, have developed various mechanisms for linking their front and hind wings to produce two, rather than four, flight surfaces that beat together. The true flies have lost one pair of wings altogether.

FRINGED WINGS
Small insects have great difficulty flying. The fringe of scales on this magnified mosquito wing probably act like the flaps, or airfoils, on an airplane wing, and help reduce the "drag." Very small insects often have narrow wings with even longer fringes.

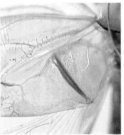 

CRICKET SONGS
Male crickets produce songs with their specially adapted front wings. The base of the left front wing (above left) has a rigid file that is scraped against a special drumlike area, or mirror, on the right front wing (above right). This mirror amplifies the sound to attract female crickets many yards away.

Antenna

Eye

1 BEFORE TAKEOFF
Like any airplane, a large insect such as this cockchafer beetle (*Melolontha melolontha*) must warm up its engines before flying. Before taking to the air, beetles will often open and shut their wing cases several times to check that they are in good working order. It is not unusual to see moths rapidly vibrating their wings before takeoff to warm up their flight muscles.

Antenna spread to sense the air currents

Claws on feet enable beetle to grip plant firmly, ready for takeoff

Wing cases start to open

Hind wings folded beneath wing cases

2 UNFASTEN THE WINGS
The hardened wing cases of the front wings are separated as the cockchafer prepares to take off from the top of the plant. The antennae are spread to check the air currents.

Wing cases, or elytra, protect the beetle's more delicate hind wings, which are folded up underneath (pp. 6–7)

Abdomen

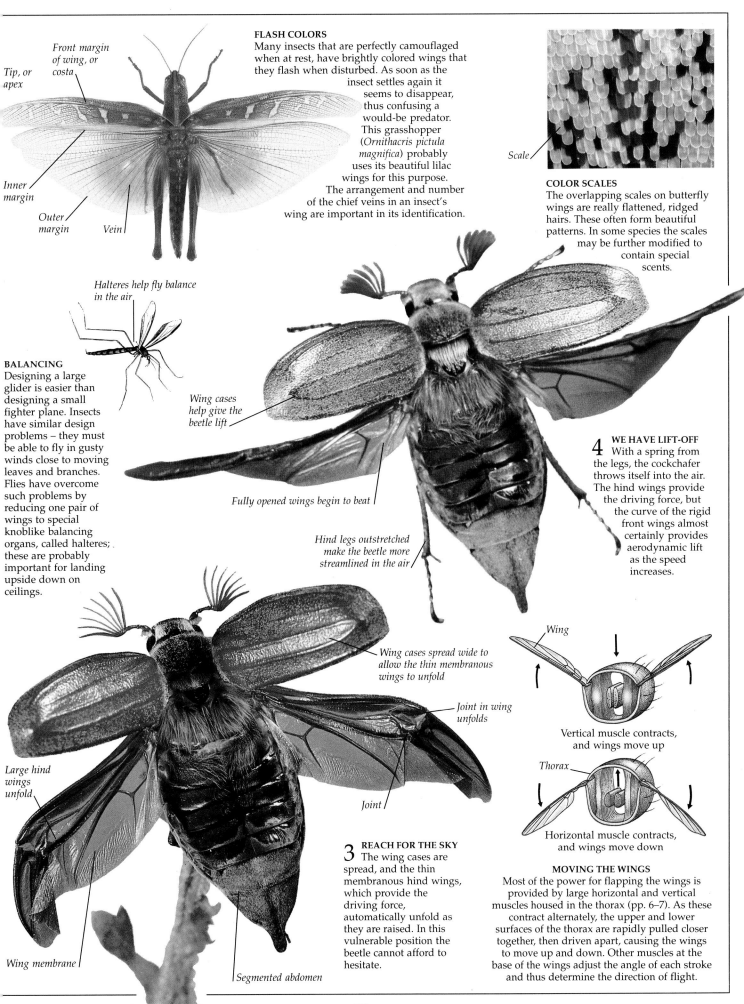

FLASH COLORS
Many insects that are perfectly camouflaged when at rest, have brightly colored wings that they flash when disturbed. As soon as the insect settles again it seems to disappear, thus confusing a would-be predator. This grasshopper (*Ornithacris pictula magnifica*) probably uses its beautiful lilac wings for this purpose. The arrangement and number of the chief veins in an insect's wing are important in its identification.

Front margin of wing, or costa

Tip, or apex

Inner margin

Outer margin

Vein

Scale

COLOR SCALES
The overlapping scales on butterfly wings are really flattened, ridged hairs. These often form beautiful patterns. In some species the scales may be further modified to contain special scents.

Halteres help fly balance in the air

BALANCING
Designing a large glider is easier than designing a small fighter plane. Insects have similar design problems – they must be able to fly in gusty winds close to moving leaves and branches. Flies have overcome such problems by reducing one pair of wings to special knoblike balancing organs, called halteres; these are probably important for landing upside down on ceilings.

Wing cases help give the beetle lift

Fully opened wings begin to beat

Hind legs outstretched make the beetle more streamlined in the air

4 WE HAVE LIFT-OFF
With a spring from the legs, the cockchafer throws itself into the air. The hind wings provide the driving force, but the curve of the rigid front wings almost certainly provides aerodynamic lift as the speed increases.

Wing cases spread wide to allow the thin membranous wings to unfold

Joint in wing unfolds

Large hind wings unfold

Joint

Wing

Vertical muscle contracts, and wings move up

Thorax

Horizontal muscle contracts, and wings move down

MOVING THE WINGS
Most of the power for flapping the wings is provided by large horizontal and vertical muscles housed in the thorax (pp. 6–7). As these contract alternately, the upper and lower surfaces of the thorax are rapidly pulled closer together, then driven apart, causing the wings to move up and down. Other muscles at the base of the wings adjust the angle of each stroke and thus determine the direction of flight.

3 REACH FOR THE SKY
The wing cases are spread, and the thin membranous hind wings, which provide the driving force, automatically unfold as they are raised. In this vulnerable position the beetle cannot afford to hesitate.

Wing membrane

Segmented abdomen

Through an insect's eyes

I IS VERY DIFFICULT to explain what is meant by color to someone who has never been able to see. But it is far more difficult to understand what color, or even sight, means to an insect. Insects have acute senses that humans do not share. Many insects can smell particular odors over great distances. Others can detect vibrations and hear sounds that are inaudible to people. But we cannot know what sort of image insects have of the world through their eyes. We know that a large bee sitting on a post can see a person move several yards away – but does it just see a moving shape, or can it perceive that the moving object is a human and not a horse? We know some bugs can see, or are particularly attracted to, ultraviolet light and the color yellow, but are not attracted to blue or red. But do they see colors, or shades of black and white? Different insects have evolved solutions to different problems. Dragonflies can catch mosquitos in flight at dusk, when it is too dark for these small flies to be seen by humans; but does the dragonfly see them, or does it respond to their sound and movement? The subject of insect senses is full of such questions.

LIGHT ATTRACTION
At night, bright lights attract many insects. It seems that night-flying insects navigate by keeping the natural light of the moon at a constant angle to their eyes. An artificial light is treated in the same way; the insects fly toward the light in a straight line but when they reach it they circle around it continuously.

Three simple eyes, or ocelli, are probably sensitive to light

Natural light

Ultraviolet light

Sense hairs all over the head give the wasp extra information about its surroundings

Segmented antennae detect odors and measure the size of the cells during nest building

BEAUTY LIES IN THE EYES OF THE BEHOLDER
The eyes of many insects register things that humans cannot see. These two brimstone butterflies have been photographed in natural light (left) and in ultraviolet light (right). Insects possibly do not see a yellow butterfly with four orange spots, but a gray insect with two large dark gray areas. Many insect-pollinated flowers rely on ultraviolet vision to attract pollinating bees (pp. 42–43); the position of the nectar within the flower is indicated by lines called honey guides, which are visible only in ultraviolet light.

A WASPISH FACE
The head of a typical insect has a pair of large compound eyes as well as three simple eyes on top. The compound eyes of this wasp (*Vespula vulgaris*) extend low down on the cheeks toward the jaws but are not developed on the part of the face across which the antennae usually lie. The segmented antennae are important not just to detect odors but also to measure the size and shape of each new cell in the nest as it is built (pp. 50–51). The powerful jaws are the hands and tools of a wasp and are used to cut up food, to dig with, and to lay down new nest material. The brilliant yellow and black pattern warns other animals that this insect has a dangerous sting.

Powerful jaws are used for digging, cutting up food, and laying down new nest material

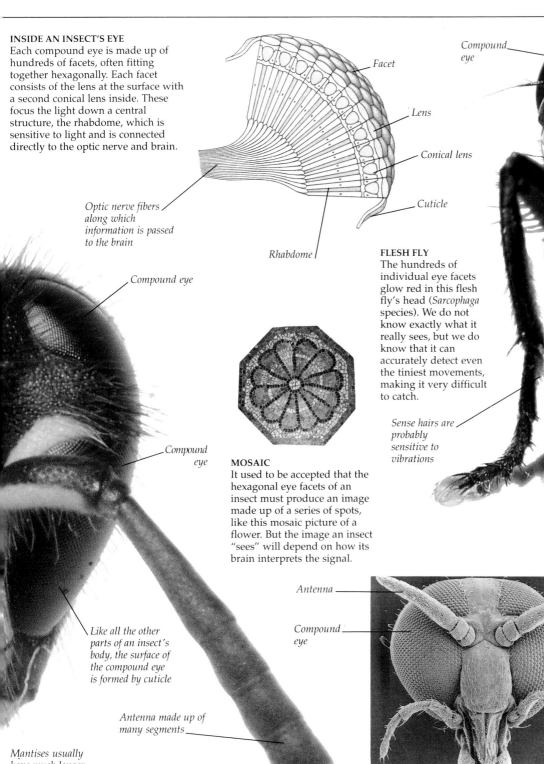

INSIDE AN INSECT'S EYE

Each compound eye is made up of hundreds of facets, often fitting together hexagonally. Each facet consists of the lens at the surface with a second conical lens inside. These focus the light down a central structure, the rhabdome, which is sensitive to light and is connected directly to the optic nerve and brain.

Facet

Lens

Conical lens

Cuticle

Optic nerve fibers along which information is passed to the brain

Rhabdome

Compound eye

FLESH FLY

The hundreds of individual eye facets glow red in this flesh fly's head (*Sarcophaga* species). We do not know exactly what it really sees, but we do know that it can accurately detect even the tiniest movements, making it very difficult to catch.

Sense hairs are probably sensitive to vibrations

Compound eye

Compound eye

MOSAIC

It used to be accepted that the hexagonal eye facets of an insect must produce an image made up of a series of spots, like this mosaic picture of a flower. But the image an insect "sees" will depend on how its brain interprets the signal.

Between the claws of a fly's foot is a sucker-like pad (p. 18) that enables the fly to walk upside down on smooth surfaces

Like all the other parts of an insect's body, the surface of the compound eye is formed by cuticle

Antenna

Compound eye

Antenna made up of many segments

Mantises usually have much longer antennae than these

BLACKFLY EYES

This South American bloodsucking fly (*Simulium bipunctatum*) is tiny, scarcely 0.08 in (2 mm) long. The head (above) has been photo-graphed with an electron microscope to show the large, many-faceted compound eyes extending around the bases of the antennae. The photograph on the right shows just one of the individual eyes, or facets, of the blackfly eye, magnified 4,000 times. The surface of each facet is finely sculptured, quite different from the diagram shown above. What does the blackfly "see" through its hundreds of tiny eyes, each one covered in tiny ridges and peglike tubercles?

I'M WATCHING YOU

The face of a praying mantis gives the impression of being constantly alert. The individual eyes, or facets, that combine to form each compound eye are very small, and a mantis will respond quickly to small movements. It often nods and tilts its head from side to side as it sizes up its potential prey and estimates the distance for its attack.

Touch, smell, and hearing

FOR MANY INSECTS the world is probably a pattern of smells and tastes. Most insects have eyes, but sight is not as important to them as it is to humans in understanding the world around them. Ants lay down a chemical trail and constantly touch each other to pass on their nest odor. Alarm chemicals are produced by many insects, so that the other members of a colony quickly respond. Female moths produce chemicals capable of attracting males from great distances. Dung beetles can locate fresh dung within 60 seconds of its being produced. Some insects, such as bark beetles, produce chemicals that attract members of the same species; this causes them to group together on a suitable tree. Other species, such as the common apple maggot, produce chemicals to prevent a second female from laying eggs on a fruit that is already occupied. This insect world of smells and tastes also includes vibrations and sounds undetected by humans. Such vibrations may be detected by insects through well-formed "ears" as on the front legs of crickets and on the abdomen of grasshoppers and cicadas, or they may be picked up through the legs and antennae.

FEATHERY FEELERS
This feather-like structure is the highly sensitive antenna of a male moth. The central rod has many side, or lateral, branches, each of which is covered in tiny sensory hairs.

Antenna

Simianellus cyaneicollis at about five times life size

BEETLE ANTLERS
It is not known for certain why both male and female of this Indian beetle have these remarkable antler-like antennae. In life, the antennae are usually held back along the body with the branches closed.

Biting jaws

Weevil's head (*Cyrtotrachelus* species) at about seven times life size

Clubbed tip is covered in sensory hairs

Rostrum used for drilling into plant seeds and stems

Elbowed antenna

NOSY WEEVIL
The biting jaws of a weevil are at the end of the long snout, or rostrum, in front of the eyes (p. 30). On either side of the rostrum is an "elbowed" antenna. The flattened surface of the club at the end of the antennae is covered with sensory hairs, which the weevil uses to explore the surface it is feeding on or into which it is drilling with its rostrum.

Eye

Head swivels inside thorax

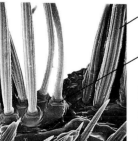

Each hair is ridged

Ball and socket joint

MAGNIFIED HAIRS
The hairs on an insect's body are often not just simple and "hairlike," which becomes apparent when they are magnified 1,000 times. These hairs, from around the mouth of a carpet beetle larva, each have their own "ball and socket" joint at the base and ridged sides. Each hair is probably sensitive to vibrations.

Butterfly antenna

Butterfly antenna, magnified 2,000 times

SIMPLY ANTENNAE?
This is part of the antenna of a butterfly, with one of the segments magnified 2,000 times. The surface is covered with intricate patterns of tiny sensitive pegs, or tubercles, and there are thin areas of cuticle (pp. 6–7) with tiny scent-sensitive hairs.

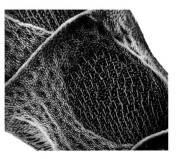

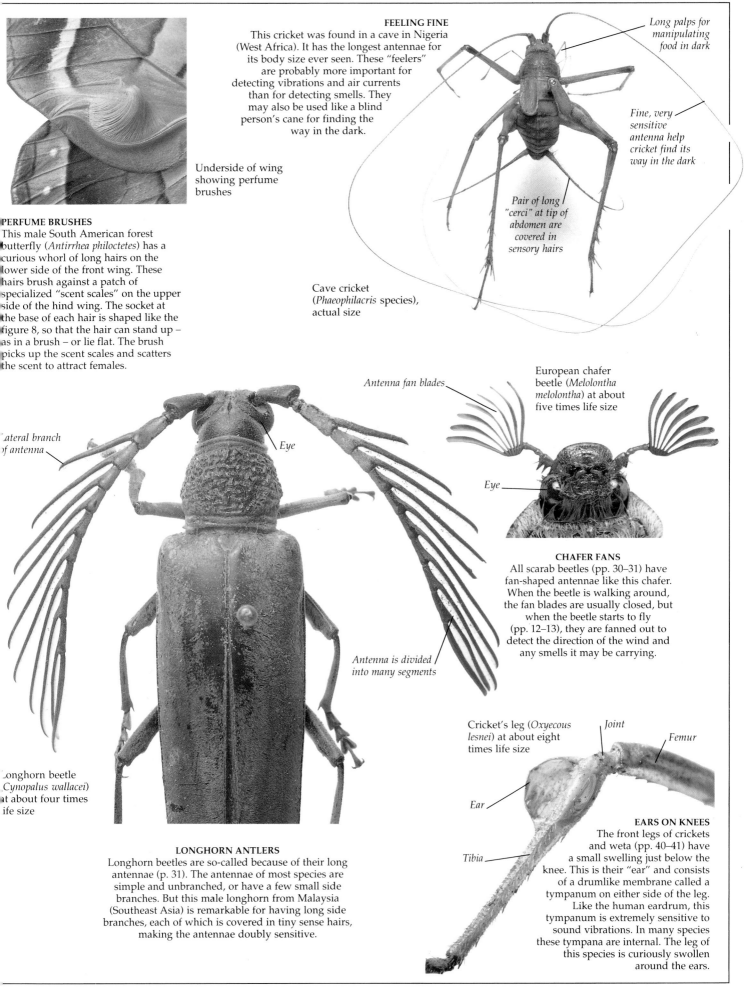

FEELING FINE
This cricket was found in a cave in Nigeria (West Africa). It has the longest antennae for its body size ever seen. These "feelers" are probably more important for detecting vibrations and air currents than for detecting smells. They may also be used like a blind person's cane for finding the way in the dark.

Long palps for manipulating food in dark

Fine, very sensitive antenna help cricket find its way in the dark

Pair of long "cerci" at tip of abdomen are covered in sensory hairs

Cave cricket (*Phaeophilacris* species), actual size

Underside of wing showing perfume brushes

PERFUME BRUSHES
This male South American forest butterfly (*Antirrhea philoctetes*) has a curious whorl of long hairs on the lower side of the front wing. These hairs brush against a patch of specialized "scent scales" on the upper side of the hind wing. The socket at the base of each hair is shaped like the figure 8, so that the hair can stand up – as in a brush – or lie flat. The brush picks up the scent scales and scatters the scent to attract females.

Antenna fan blades

European chafer beetle (*Melolontha melolontha*) at about five times life size

Eye

CHAFER FANS
All scarab beetles (pp. 30–31) have fan-shaped antennae like this chafer. When the beetle is walking around, the fan blades are usually closed, but when the beetle starts to fly (pp. 12–13), they are fanned out to detect the direction of the wind and any smells it may be carrying.

Lateral branch of antenna

Eye

Antenna is divided into many segments

Longhorn beetle (*Cynopalus wallacei*) at about four times life size

LONGHORN ANTLERS
Longhorn beetles are so-called because of their long antennae (p. 31). The antennae of most species are simple and unbranched, or have a few small side branches. But this male longhorn from Malaysia (Southeast Asia) is remarkable for having long side branches, each of which is covered in tiny sense hairs, making the antennae doubly sensitive.

Cricket's leg (*Oxyecous lesnei*) at about eight times life size

Joint

Femur

Ear

Tibia

EARS ON KNEES
The front legs of crickets and weta (pp. 40–41) have a small swelling just below the knee. This is their "ear" and consists of a drumlike membrane called a tympanum on either side of the leg. Like the human eardrum, this tympanum is extremely sensitive to sound vibrations. In many species these tympana are internal. The leg of this species is curiously swollen around the ears.

Legwork

LEGS ARE IMPORTANT to most creatures for walking, running, and jumping, as well as for generally keeping the body off the ground. Insects have found even more uses for their legs. Bees (pp. 58–59) have little brushes and baskets on their legs for collecting and storing pollen (pp. 42–43). Grasshoppers can "sing" with their legs by rubbing a small file on their hind legs against their front wings. Crickets have ears on their knees, and many insects' legs are modified for fighting or for holding on to the opposite sex when mating. Some water insects (pp. 48–49) have flattened legs with long hairs that work like paddles or oars; others have long, delicate, stilt-like legs for walking on the surface without sinking. All insects have six jointed legs, and each leg has four main parts. At the top is the coxa, which joins the leg to the thorax; then comes the thigh, or femur; and the lower leg, or tibia. At the tip of the leg is the tarsus, which usually has two claws and sometimes has a pad in between, enabling the insect to climb on almost any surface, however smooth.

CLEANING LEGS
Cleaning legs

Flies are covered in hairs, which must be cleaned and groomed regularly if the insect is to fly effectively. The feet of houseflies have special pads between the claws that work like plastic wrap, enabling the insect to walk upside down on smooth surfaces.

Propeller-like feet can bury this cricket in seconds

Wings coiled like a spring

GOING DOWN
The strange, propeller-like feet of this desert-dwelling cricket (*Schizodactylus monstrosus*) enable it to dig a hole in sand directly beneath itself and disappear in a matter of seconds – straight down. The ends of the wings are coiled like a spring, which keeps the wings out of the way.

Hind wings tilted above body

Front legs outstretched, ready for touchdown

Front wings curved to scoop up the air

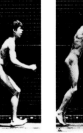

BOUNCING BOYS
This famous sequence by Muybridge (1830-1903) shows how vertebrates (p. 9) can jump, land, and jump again in one action. Insects, which have less complex muscles and joints, must usually rest for a moment between jumps.

1 TOUCHING DOWN
Landing safely is always a problem when flying. This locust (*Schistocerca gregaria*) has its legs spread wide, its hind wings tilted, and its front wings curved to catch the maximum amount of air. The wing shape of birds and airplanes is adjusted in the same way when landing, to enable them to slow down and drop gently to the ground. Locusts are particular species of grasshopper that occasionally change their behavior and form migrating swarms of thousands of millions of insects (p. 61).

Mottled markings on wings help conceal insect on the ground (pp. 44–45)

Tibia

Femur

Compound eye

2 PREPARING TO JUMP
The locust gets ready to jump again by bringing the long, slender parts of its hind legs (tibiae) close under the body near its center of gravity. The large muscles in the thicker part of the leg (femur) are attached to the tip of the tibia. When these muscles shorten, or contract, the leg is suddenly straightened, throwing the insect into the air.

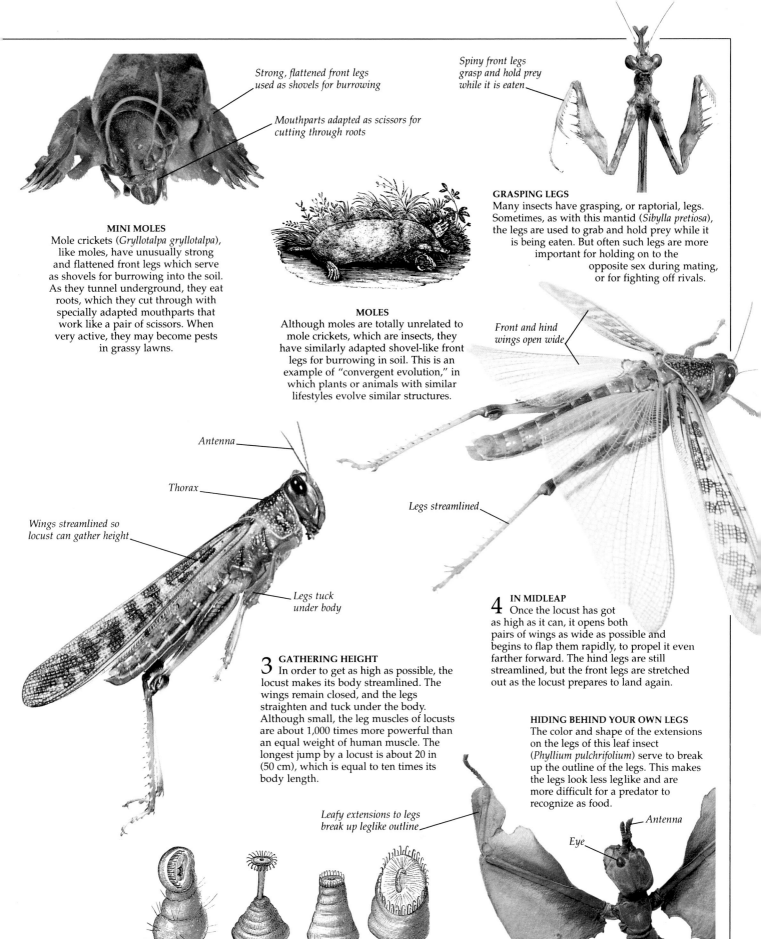

Strong, flattened front legs
used as shovels for burrowing

Mouthparts adapted as scissors for
cutting through roots

Spiny front legs
grasp and hold prey
while it is eaten

MINI MOLES
Mole crickets (*Gryllotalpa gryllotalpa*),
like moles, have unusually strong
and flattened front legs which serve
as shovels for burrowing into the soil.
As they tunnel underground, they eat
roots, which they cut through with
specially adapted mouthparts that
work like a pair of scissors. When
very active, they may become pests
in grassy lawns.

MOLES
Although moles are totally unrelated to
mole crickets, which are insects, they
have similarly adapted shovel-like front
legs for burrowing in soil. This is an
example of "convergent evolution," in
which plants or animals with similar
lifestyles evolve similar structures.

GRASPING LEGS
Many insects have grasping, or raptorial, legs.
Sometimes, as with this mantid (*Sibylla pretiosa*),
the legs are used to grab and hold prey while it
is being eaten. But often such legs are more
important for holding on to the
opposite sex during mating,
or for fighting off rivals.

Front and hind
wings open wide

Antenna

Thorax

Wings streamlined so
locust can gather height

Legs streamlined

Legs tuck
under body

3 GATHERING HEIGHT
In order to get as high as possible, the
locust makes its body streamlined. The
wings remain closed, and the legs
straighten and tuck under the body.
Although small, the leg muscles of locusts
are about 1,000 times more powerful than
an equal weight of human muscle. The
longest jump by a locust is about 20 in
(50 cm), which is equal to ten times its
body length.

4 IN MIDLEAP
Once the locust has got
as high as it can, it opens both
pairs of wings as wide as possible and
begins to flap them rapidly, to propel it even
farther forward. The hind legs are still
streamlined, but the front legs are stretched
out as the locust prepares to land again.

HIDING BEHIND YOUR OWN LEGS
The color and shape of the extensions
on the legs of this leaf insect
(*Phyllium pulchrifolium*) serve to break
up the outline of the legs. This makes
the legs look less leglike and are
more difficult for a predator to
recognize as food.

Antenna

Eye

Leafy extensions to legs
break up leglike outline

PSEUDOFEET
The "legs" on the abdomen of caterpillars are not real legs. They are
muscular extensions of the body wall, called prolegs, each with a circle
of hairs at the tip. The prolegs are important for locomotion, and the
three pairs of real legs on the thorax are used to hold the food.

Greens and browns
blend in with leafy
surroundings

Mouthparts and feeding

THE ANCESTORS OF INSECTS had three pairs of jaws on their head. In modern insects the first pair, the mandibles, remain well developed in all chewing species. The second pair, the maxillae, are smaller and modified to help push or suck food into the mouth. And the third pair are joined together to form the lower lip, or labium. But in many insects these three pairs of jaws are modified according to diet into piercing needles, long, sucking tubes, and absorbent sponges.

BUSH CRICKET
This bush cricket is feeding on part of a flower. It is holding the plant with its front legs while the large and powerful sawlike mandibles chew it up. Crickets also eat other insects – even their own young.

FLEA BITES
This old engraving is not accurate, but it shows that fleas have a strong sucking tube surrounded by two pairs of palps, or sensory organs.

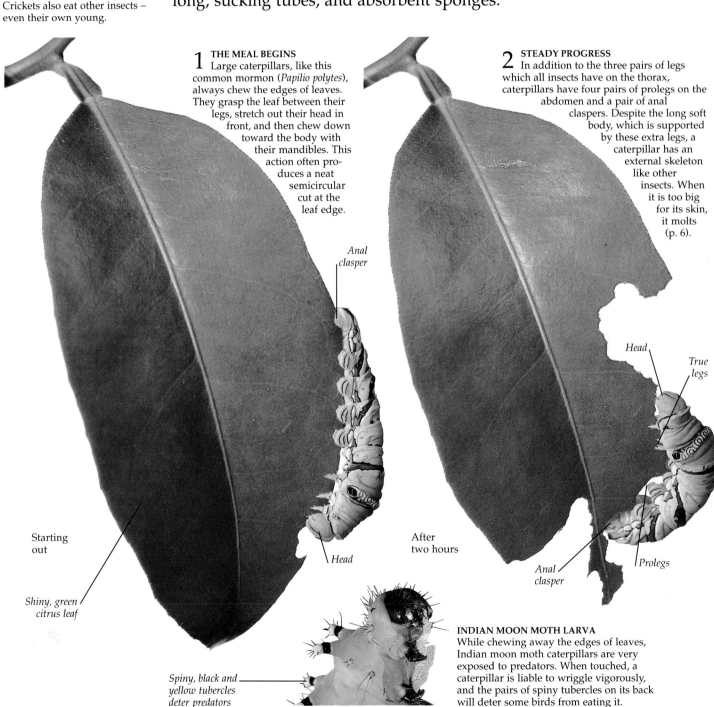

1 THE MEAL BEGINS
Large caterpillars, like this common mormon (*Papilio polytes*), always chew the edges of leaves. They grasp the leaf between their legs, stretch out their head in front, and then chew down toward the body with their mandibles. This action often produces a neat semicircular cut at the leaf edge.

Anal clasper

Starting out

Head

Shiny, green citrus leaf

Spiny, black and yellow tubercles deter predators

2 STEADY PROGRESS
In addition to the three pairs of legs which all insects have on the thorax, caterpillars have four pairs of prolegs on the abdomen and a pair of anal claspers. Despite the long soft body, which is supported by these extra legs, a caterpillar has an external skeleton like other insects. When it is too big for its skin, it molts (p. 6).

Head

True legs

After two hours

Anal clasper

Prolegs

INDIAN MOON MOTH LARVA
While chewing away the edges of leaves, Indian moon moth caterpillars are very exposed to predators. When touched, a caterpillar is liable to wriggle vigorously, and the pairs of spiny tubercles on its back will deter some birds from eating it.

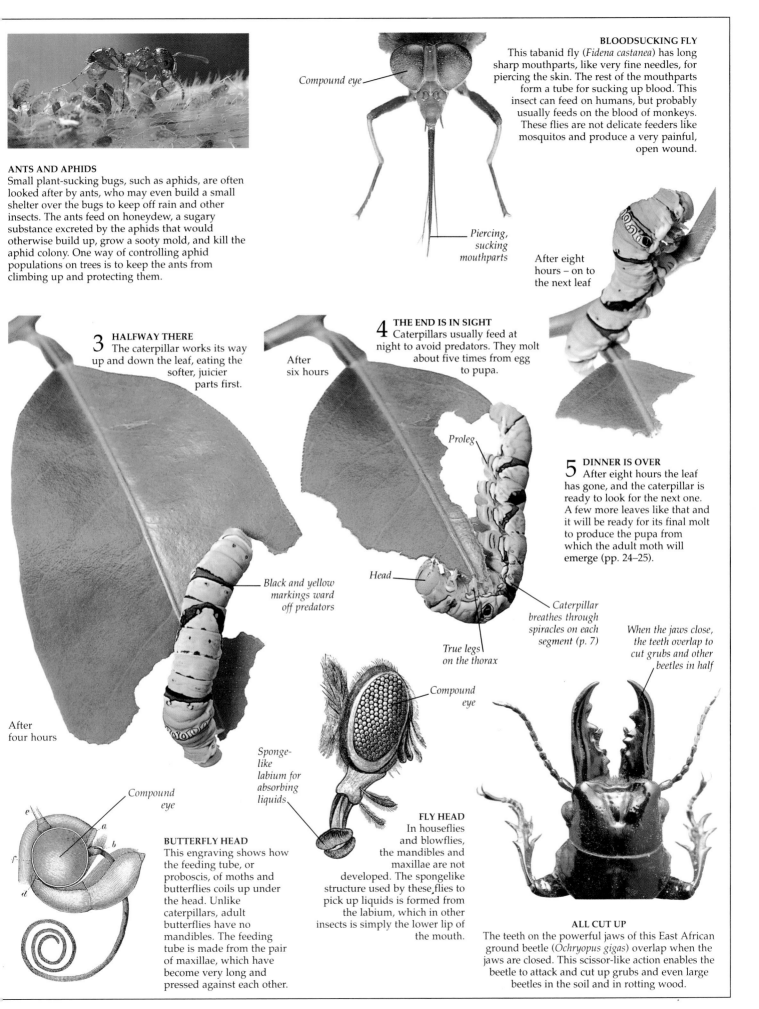

ANTS AND APHIDS
Small plant-sucking bugs, such as aphids, are often looked after by ants, who may even build a small shelter over the bugs to keep off rain and other insects. The ants feed on honeydew, a sugary substance excreted by the aphids that would otherwise build up, grow a sooty mold, and kill the aphid colony. One way of controlling aphid populations on trees is to keep the ants from climbing up and protecting them.

BLOODSUCKING FLY
This tabanid fly (*Fidena castanea*) has long sharp mouthparts, like very fine needles, for piercing the skin. The rest of the mouthparts form a tube for sucking up blood. This insect can feed on humans, but probably usually feeds on the blood of monkeys. These flies are not delicate feeders like mosquitos and produce a very painful, open wound.

Compound eye

Piercing, sucking mouthparts

After eight hours – on to the next leaf

3 HALFWAY THERE
The caterpillar works its way up and down the leaf, eating the softer, juicier parts first.

After six hours

4 THE END IS IN SIGHT
Caterpillars usually feed at night to avoid predators. They molt about five times from egg to pupa.

Proleg

5 DINNER IS OVER
After eight hours the leaf has gone, and the caterpillar is ready to look for the next one. A few more leaves like that and it will be ready for its final molt to produce the pupa from which the adult moth will emerge (pp. 24–25).

Head

Black and yellow markings ward off predators

Caterpillar breathes through spiracles on each segment (p. 7)

True legs on the thorax

When the jaws close, the teeth overlap to cut grubs and other beetles in half

After four hours

Compound eye

Compound eye

Sponge-like labium for absorbing liquids

BUTTERFLY HEAD
This engraving shows how the feeding tube, or proboscis, of moths and butterflies coils up under the head. Unlike caterpillars, adult butterflies have no mandibles. The feeding tube is made from the pair of maxillae, which have become very long and pressed against each other.

FLY HEAD
In houseflies and blowflies, the mandibles and maxillae are not developed. The spongelike structure used by these flies to pick up liquids is formed from the labium, which in other insects is simply the lower lip of the mouth.

ALL CUT UP
The teeth on the powerful jaws of this East African ground beetle (*Ochryopus gigas*) overlap when the jaws are closed. This scissor-like action enables the beetle to attack and cut up grubs and even large beetles in the soil and in rotting wood.

Battling beetles

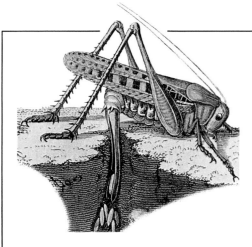

IN WARM WEATHER, if its host plant is healthy, an aphid can produce 50 offspring in a week, each of which will be mature one week later. At this rate of breeding the world could be knee-deep in aphids within a few weeks – but this does not happen. The number of plants necessary to feed large insect populations is limited, and this lack of resources together with hungry predators limits the number of insects. Despite this, a large swarm of locusts will include many thousands of millions of individuals. Some insects, such as those that feed on dead wood, compete for food and breeding sites. In many such insects, the males may have large horns or big jaws to fight off rival males and lay claim to a dead branch on which to mate and breed.

Femur

Tibia

Tarsus

Let's see who's
boss around here!

*Antlerlike
jaws*

*Antenna outstretched to pick
up as much information as
possible about the other beetle*

Thorax

1 EYEING UP THE OPPOSITION
Stag beetles, like these two from Europe (*Lucanus cervus*), get their name from the large branched "horns" of the male. These are really greatly enlarged jaws that are used for fighting, much like the antlers of a real stag. A male defends his territory, usually at dusk, by adopting a threatening position.

*Hard, black,
protective
wing case*

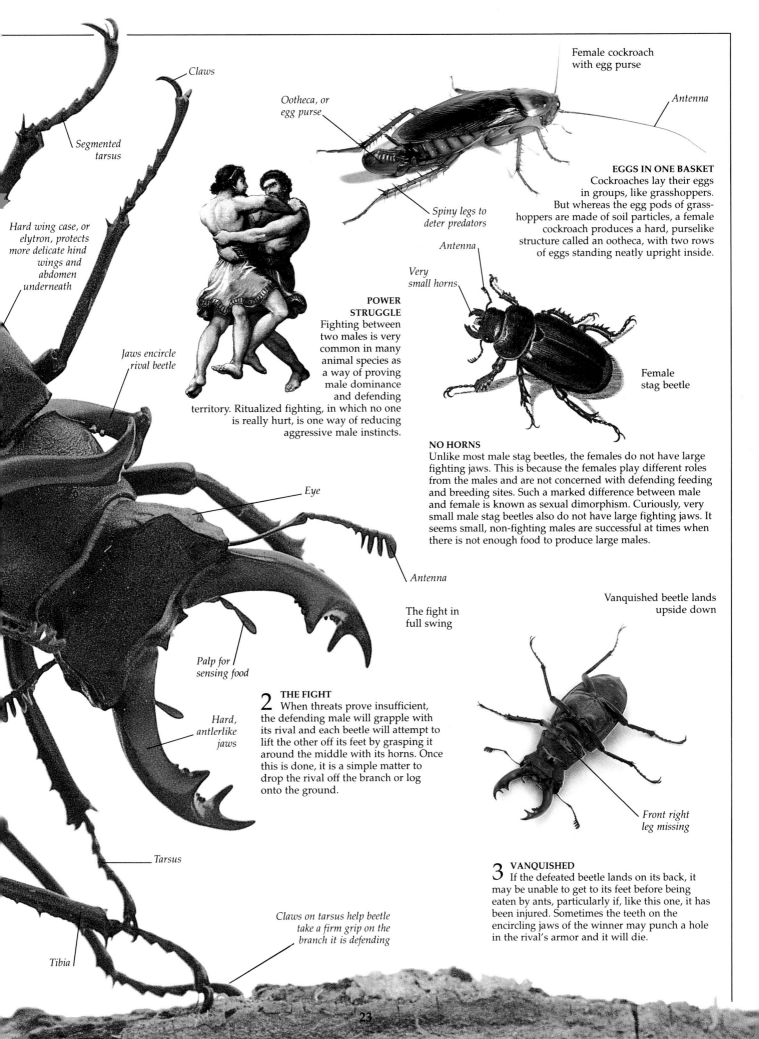

Claws

Segmented
tarsus

Hard wing case, or
elytron, protects
more delicate hind
wings and
abdomen
underneath

Jaws encircle
rival beetle

Ootheca, or
egg purse

Female cockroach
with egg purse

Antenna

Spiny legs to
deter predators

EGGS IN ONE BASKET
Cockroaches lay their eggs
in groups, like grasshoppers.
But whereas the egg pods of grasshoppers are made of soil particles, a female
cockroach produces a hard, purselike
structure called an ootheca, with two rows
of eggs standing neatly upright inside.

Antenna

Very
small horns

Female
stag beetle

**POWER
STRUGGLE**
Fighting between
two males is very
common in many
animal species as
a way of proving
male dominance
and defending
territory. Ritualized fighting, in which no one
is really hurt, is one way of reducing
aggressive male instincts.

NO HORNS
Unlike most male stag beetles, the females do not have large
fighting jaws. This is because the females play different roles
from the males and are not concerned with defending feeding
and breeding sites. Such a marked difference between male
and female is known as sexual dimorphism. Curiously, very
small male stag beetles also do not have large fighting jaws. It
seems small, non-fighting males are successful at times when
there is not enough food to produce large males.

Eye

Antenna

The fight in
full swing

Vanquished beetle lands
upside down

Palp for
sensing food

Hard,
antlerlike
jaws

2 THE FIGHT
When threats prove insufficient,
the defending male will grapple with
its rival and each beetle will attempt to
lift the other off its feet by grasping it
around the middle with its horns. Once
this is done, it is a simple matter to
drop the rival off the branch or log
onto the ground.

Front right
leg missing

Tarsus

3 VANQUISHED
If the defeated beetle lands on its back, it
may be unable to get to its feet before being
eaten by ants, particularly if, like this one, it has
been injured. Sometimes the teeth on the
encircling jaws of the winner may punch a hole
in the rival's armor and it will die.

Claws on tarsus help beetle
take a firm grip on the
branch it is defending

Tibia

Complete metamorphosis

METAMORPHOSIS MEANS "change of body form and appearance." The most advanced insects have a complex life cycle involving "complete" metamorphosis. The eggs hatch to produce larvae (caterpillars, grubs, or maggots) that are quite unlike adult insects in both form and appearance. The larvae grow and molt several times (pp. 6–7), finally producing a pupa (chrysalis). Inside the pupa the whole body is reorganized, and a winged adult is produced. This type of life cycle enables the larvae to specialize in feeding, and the adults to specialize in breeding and looking for new sites. Wasps, bees, ants, flies, beetles, butterflies and moths, caddis flies, fleas, lacewings, and scorpion flies all undergo complete metamorphosis. But not all insects obey the rules: the adults of some species of beetle look like larvae; some female mountain moths are wingless; and some flies have no adults because each larva can produce many more larvae inside its body.

MATING
Mexican bean beetles (*Epilachna varivestis*) are a species of plant-feeding ladybird beetle. The adult males and females look very similar and mate frequently.

EGGS
Female Mexican bean beetles lay their eggs in groups of about 50 on the underside of leaves where they are well protected. Each egg stands on end and takes about a week to hatch.

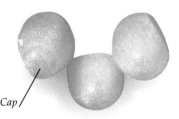

Larva emerges

Cap

1 EGG HATCHES
Even eggs have to breathe. Around the top of each egg is a ring of pores which allow air to reach the developing larva inside. About a week after the egg has been laid, the cap at the top is broken or chewed off, and the larva emerges.

Old larval skin

New pupal skin

4 ABOUT TO CHANGE
When the larva has eaten enough food, it attaches itself to the underside of a damaged, netted leaf, ready to pupate. The larval skin is shed, and soft new pupal skin forms beneath it. This quickly hardens.

Larva feeding on plant shoot

EATING LEAVES
Mexican bean beetles feed on leaves both as larvae and as adults. Because they eat only the fleshy parts in between the veins, the leaf ends up netted and lacy.

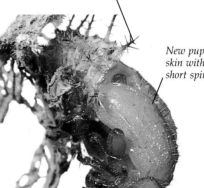

Old larval skin with long spines

New pupal skin with short spines

Dead, lacy leaves on which larvae have fed.

5 RESTING
A pupa is often called a "resting stage." But there will be no rest for all the cells in the body. All the muscles, nerves, and other structures are dissolved, and new limbs, with new muscles and nerves, are formed. In this picture, the smooth yellow of the adult beetle's wing cases and the first segment of the thorax can be seen through the thin, spiny skin of the pupa.

Larval skin

Larval skin splits

Head emerges first

6 READY TO FEED
The thin, spiny pupal skin splits along the underside, and the smooth young adult slowly draws itself free, head first. It takes the young beetle about one hour from the splitting of the pupal skin to free itself fully.

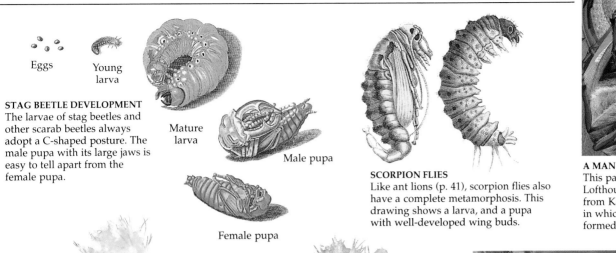

STAG BEETLE DEVELOPMENT

The larvae of stag beetles and other scarab beetles always adopt a C-shaped posture. The male pupa with its large jaws is easy to tell apart from the female pupa.

Eggs

Young larva

Mature larva

Male pupa

Female pupa

SCORPION FLIES

Like ant lions (p. 41), scorpion flies also have a complete metamorphosis. This drawing shows a larva, and a pupa with well-developed wing buds.

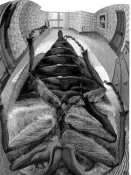

A MAN TRANSFORMED

This painting by Barbara Lofthouse depicts a scene from Kafka's *Metamorphosis*, in which a man is transformed into an insect.

Red spots are associated with simple eyes

2 LARVA EMERGES

As the soft-spined larva crawls out of its egg, three red pigment spots can be seen on either side of the head. Larvae do not have compound eyes, like adults, and these spots are associated with simple eyes.

3 A FIRST MEAL

In many insect species, as soon as a young larva is free from its egg, it turns around and eats the shell, which is thought to contain valuable nutrients. The soft spines on the surface of the larva quickly harden.

PROTECTION FROM PARASITES

The spines on the surface of the larvae are branched, with hard, pointed tips. Spines like this are found on the larvae of all plant-feeding ladybirds, but not on any of the more common predatory species. The spines make the larvae unpleasant to birds and may prevent parasites from laying eggs.

Old larval skin remains attached to leaf

7 NO SPOTS

Immediately after emerging, the young beetle is yellow and has no spots, although the wing cases quickly harden. Before the beetle can fly, there then follows a crucial stage lasting two to three hours, where the young beetle holds its wing cases up and expands the wings below to allow them to dry.

Young adult

8 ONE MORE PEST

After about 24 hours the adult spots will appear on the wing cases, but the copper color takes seven to ten days to develop fully. About 100 years ago this species spread slowly northward from Mexico on plots of phaseolus beans. Then in 1918 it was accidentally imported to the eastern United States and spread rapidly toward Canada. Today it is a serious pest of bean crops in North and Central America, but it cannot live in central areas because of the harsher winters.

Incomplete metamorphosis

THE MOST ADVANCED INSECTS undergo complete metamorphosis (pp. 24–25), in which the body form is relatively quickly transformed from larva to adult during a pupal stage. But a gradual transformation through a series of stages, in which the nymphs look progressively more like adults, must have been the life cycle of the original primitive insects. This "incomplete" metamorphosis is found in grasshoppers, cockroaches, termites, mayflies, dragonflies, and true bugs. Very young nymphs show no signs of wings, but older nymphs have shorter or longer "buds" on the thorax, inside which the adult wings are developing. At each molt (pp. 6–7) these wing buds get longer, until finally a nymph molts and an adult emerges. The nymphs of some insects, like the damselfly shown over the next four pages, live underwater, surfacing only when it is time for the winged adult to emerge.

Male

Sperm deposited here

Female

LOVE HEARTS
Male damselflies transfer their sperm to a structure on the lower surface of the abdomen, near their back legs. They clasp the female's neck using the tip of their abdomen, and the female then raises her own abdomen to collect the sperm. They may fly together in this tandem position for some time, often forming a heart shape with the male's head down at the tip and the female's head at the top of the heart.

Eye

Water flea

Mask

NYMPH FEEDING
The mask (p. 49), which is shot out to capture prey, can be seen here holding a water flea on which the damselfly nymph is feeding.

YOUNG NYMPH
The time from egg to adult may take a few months or as long as three years depending on the species. The nymphs usually molt (p. 6) about 12 times, and the youngest stages show no signs of wing buds. The young nymphs are often transparent to help them hide from predators.

This young nymph has lost one of its gills – it should have three

Wing buds

Mature nymph

Gills

MATURE NYMPH
When fully grown, a nymph is often colored in a way that enables it to hide both from its prey and from predatory fish. The wing buds can be seen extending from the thorax over the first three segments of the abdomen.

EARWIGS
Female earwigs are known to show a primitive type of social behavior. They sometimes dig a small hole in which to lay their eggs and then remain with the eggs and protect them. If the eggs are deliberately scattered, the female earwig will gather them up again. Even when the young nymphs emerge, the female remains with them until they are ready to go off and fend for themselves.

BREATHING UNDER WATER
Dragonfly and damselfly nymphs absorb oxygen and get rid of carbon dioxide in the same way that fish do – by means of gills. But, unlike a fish, the gills of a damselfly nymph are not on the head, but in the form of three fan-shaped structures on the tail. Just how necessary these are for breathing is not quite certain because they are often bitten off by predators, although they do grow back again. Perhaps the gills have an important decoy function in diverting the attack of a predator away from the head of a nymph.

The mature nymph crawls up a stem out of the water, where the adult will emerge

The adult emerges

Although the damselfly nymph lives under water, and the adult is able to fly, the structure of the adult can clearly be seen in the mature nymph. The flight muscles and deep thorax are there, but the body and wings must become longer, and the nymphal mask must be shed from the head. These changes have all been prepared within the nymph underwater. Once it has crawled up into the air, it must change to an adult and fly quickly, usually in about two hours, or it will be eaten by some other animal.

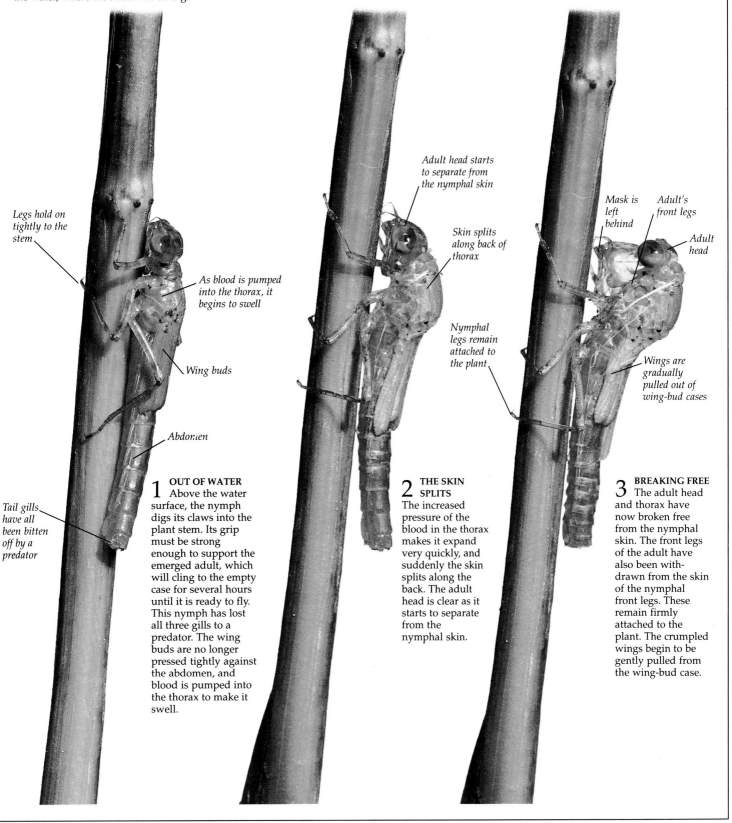

Legs hold on tightly to the stem

As blood is pumped into the thorax, it begins to swell

Wing buds

Abdomen

Tail gills have all been bitten off by a predator

Adult head starts to separate from the nymphal skin

Skin splits along back of thorax

Nymphal legs remain attached to the plant

Mask is left behind

Adult's front legs

Adult head

Wings are gradually pulled out of wing-bud cases

1 OUT OF WATER
Above the water surface, the nymph digs its claws into the plant stem. Its grip must be strong enough to support the emerged adult, which will cling to the empty case for several hours until it is ready to fly. This nymph has lost all three gills to a predator. The wing buds are no longer pressed tightly against the abdomen, and blood is pumped into the thorax to make it swell.

2 THE SKIN SPLITS
The increased pressure of the blood in the thorax makes it expand very quickly, and suddenly the skin splits along the back. The adult head is clear as it starts to separate from the nymphal skin.

3 BREAKING FREE
The adult head and thorax have now broken free from the nymphal skin. The front legs of the adult have also been withdrawn from the skin of the nymphal front legs. These remain firmly attached to the plant. The crumpled wings begin to be gently pulled from the wing-bud case.

27

Continued on next page

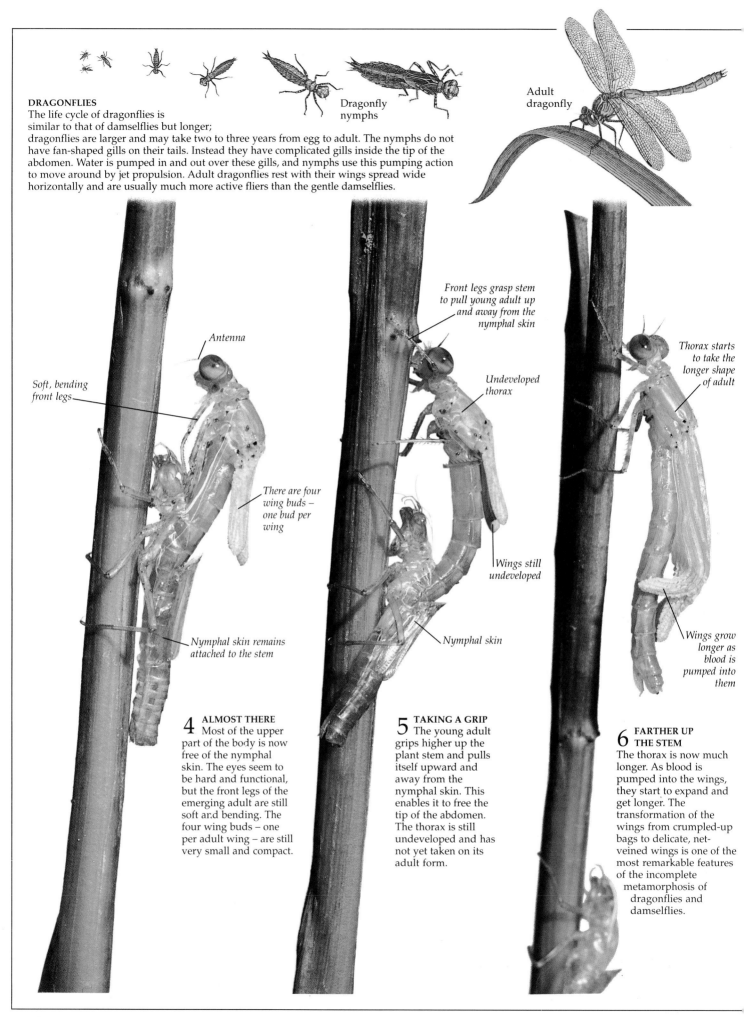

DRAGONFLIES

The life cycle of dragonflies is similar to that of damselflies but longer; dragonflies are larger and may take two to three years from egg to adult. The nymphs do not have fan-shaped gills on their tails. Instead they have complicated gills inside the tip of the abdomen. Water is pumped in and out over these gills, and nymphs use this pumping action to move around by jet propulsion. Adult dragonflies rest with their wings spread wide horizontally and are usually much more active fliers than the gentle damselflies.

Dragonfly nymphs

Adult dragonfly

Antenna

Soft, bending front legs

There are four wing buds – one bud per wing

Nymphal skin remains attached to the stem

Front legs grasp stem to pull young adult up and away from the nymphal skin

Undeveloped thorax

Wings still undeveloped

Nymphal skin

Thorax starts to take the longer shape of adult

Wings grow longer as blood is pumped into them

4 **ALMOST THERE**
Most of the upper part of the body is now free of the nymphal skin. The eyes seem to be hard and functional, but the front legs of the emerging adult are still soft ar.d bending. The four wing buds – one per adult wing – are still very small and compact.

5 **TAKING A GRIP**
The young adult grips higher up the plant stem and pulls itself upward and away from the nymphal skin. This enables it to free the tip of the abdomen. The thorax is still undeveloped and has not yet taken on its adult form.

6 **FARTHER UP THE STEM**
The thorax is now much longer. As blood is pumped into the wings, they start to expand and get longer. The transformation of the wings from crumpled-up bags to delicate, net-veined wings is one of the most remarkable features of the incomplete metamorphosis of dragonflies and damselflies.

Continued from previous page

DAMSELFLIES

These delicate-looking insects are found near water. They have four similarly shaped, net-veined wings, which they hold flattened together above their body when at rest. The damselfly photographed for the emergence sequence over these pages is a female of the species *Coenagrion puella*. Male and female damselflies are frequently quite different in color. In this species the females are black on the back and brilliant green along the sides; the males are blue on the back.

CLOSE-UP

This close-up photograph shows the head of an adult male damselfly. It has large compound eyes (pp. 14–15) as befits an active hunter. The legs are bunched behind the mouth for grasping and holding the insect prey while the powerful chewing mouthparts tear it to pieces.

Strong, chewing mouthparts

Large compound eye for spotting prey

Legs seize and hold prey

Thorax is still growing

Four wings are soft and easily damaged

Abdomen still growing longer

7 WINGS AT LAST
The four wings are almost fully expanded but they still look dull and are soft and easily damaged. The thorax and abdomen have still not reached their adult size.

Nymphal skin

Wings are ready for weak flight

Abdomen is longer and thinner

Drop of liquid

8 READY TO FLY
When the abdomen reaches its full length, a drop of liquid exudes from the tip. This is a female. She is now ready to fly weakly, although the wings are still rather milky in appearance. It is just two hours since she crawled out of the water as a curious nymph. The colors remain yellowish for many hours, and it will be several days before she gets her typical black and green color pattern.

Net-veined wings of mature adult

Black spot, known as a stigma

9 ADULT FEMALE
The brilliant mature colors of adult damselflies take a few days to develop.

Beetles

THERE ARE AT LEAST 300,000 different kinds of beetle, living everywhere from snowy mountaintops to scorching deserts and muddy ponds (pp. 48–49). Beetles eat all kinds of plants and animals, dead or alive, and are eaten in vast numbers by birds, lizards, and small mammals. Although they may be pests, attacking crops and devouring stores of human food, beetles also play an important role in nature by eating dead plants and animals and returning them to the soil as valuable nutrients. All beetles undergo complete metamorphosis (pp. 24–25). Their eggs hatch into grubs, some of which feed and grow for several years before pupating and becoming adults. Adult beetles are the most heavily armored of all insects. They have hardened front wings that meet in the middle to cover and protect the more delicate hind wings, which they use for flying (pp. 12–13). Beetles come in all sizes, from tiny fungus beetles smaller than a pinhead, to the giant Goliath, up to 6 in (15 cm) long.

SACRED SCARAB
The ancient Egyptians believed that the scarab rolling her ball of dung symbolized the sun god Ra rolling the sun and renewing life.

GOLIATH
The African Goliath beetle (*Goliathus cacicus*) is the heaviest beetle in the world and one of the largest flying insects. The adults may be as long as 6 in (15 cm) and weigh up to 3.4 oz (100 g). The grubs live in rotting vegetation. After the adults emerge, they fly up into the trees to feed on fruit and to mate.

Goliath beetle

Malayan frog beetle (male)

Doryphorella langsdorfi

LEAF LIFE
Leaf beetles, like the two shown above, are often brightly colored. The Malayan frog beetle (*Sagra buqueti*) uses its large hind legs to clasp the female during mating. The South American species (*Doryphorella langsdorfi*) lives and feeds on leaves.

Froglike hind legs

Jewel-like colors help conceal weevils on shiny green leaves

Lamprocyphus augustus

Hairs deter predators

Brachycerus fascicularis

Pachyrrhynchus species

Rostrum

Eupholus beccarii

Eupholus linnei

WEEVILS
Weevils are beetles that have a snout, or rostrum, with small biting jaws at the tip. Most weevils are plant feeders. Some are brilliantly colored and patterned, and others are hairy, possibly to deter predators. The middle three, from the Philippines, possibly mimic spiders (p. 46).

STAG BEETLE
The powerful-looking jaws of this shiny black male stag beetle (*Mesotopus tarandus*) from Africa are probably used for fighting (pp. 22–23).

Stag beetle

Ground beetle

Long running legs

Tiger beetle

KILLER BEETLES
Ground beetles and the closely related tiger beetles usually hunt and kill smaller insects for food. This large African species (*Anthia thoracica*) does not fly but scurries along the ground after its prey. The green tiger beetle (*Megacephala australis*) from Australia runs and flies in sunny places.

DARWIN'S BEETLE
It is said that this male stag beetle (*Chiasognathus granti*) bit the English naturalist Charles Darwin when he visited Brazil on the voyage of the HMS *Beagle*. The beetle probably uses its long spiny jaws to threaten or fight other males.

Darwin's beetle

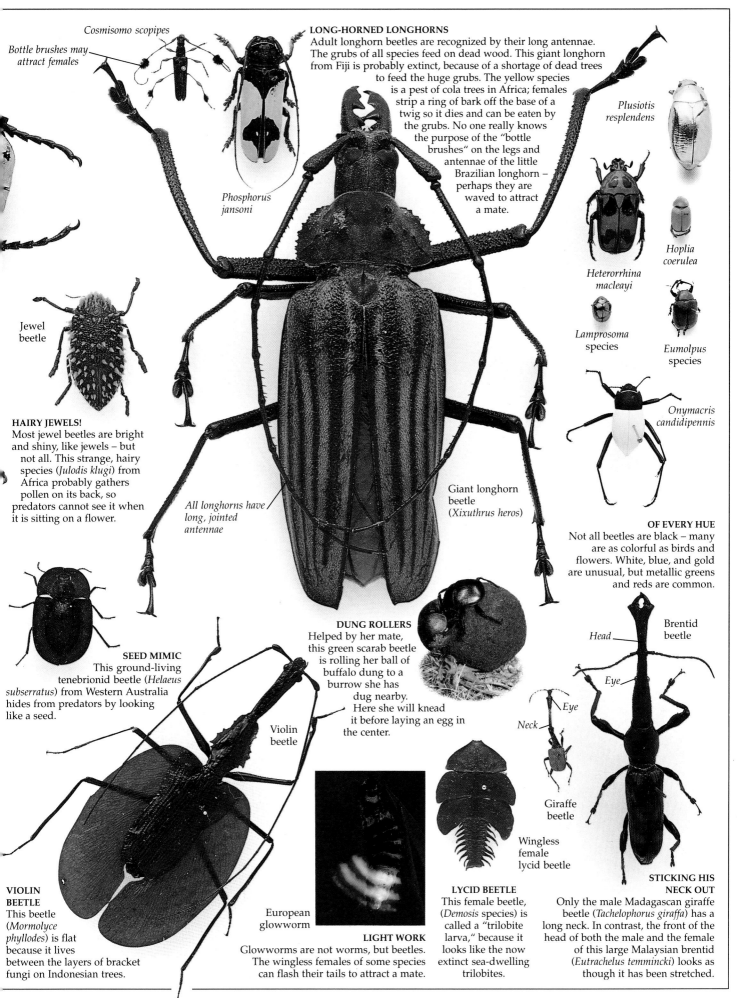

Cosmisomo scopipes

Bottle brushes may attract females

LONG-HORNED LONGHORNS
Adult longhorn beetles are recognized by their long antennae. The grubs of all species feed on dead wood. This giant longhorn from Fiji is probably extinct, because of a shortage of dead trees to feed the huge grubs. The yellow species is a pest of cola trees in Africa; females strip a ring of bark off the base of a twig so it dies and can be eaten by the grubs. No one really knows the purpose of the "bottle brushes" on the legs and antennae of the little Brazilian longhorn – perhaps they are waved to attract a mate.

Plusiotis resplendens

Phosphorus jansoni

Heterorrhina macleayi

Hoplia coerulea

Jewel beetle

Lamprosoma species

Eumolpus species

Onymacris candidipennis

HAIRY JEWELS!
Most jewel beetles are bright and shiny, like jewels – but not all. This strange, hairy species (*Julodis klugi*) from Africa probably gathers pollen on its back, so predators cannot see it when it is sitting on a flower.

All longhorns have long, jointed antennae

Giant longhorn beetle (*Xixuthrus heros*)

OF EVERY HUE
Not all beetles are black – many are as colorful as birds and flowers. White, blue, and gold are unusual, but metallic greens and reds are common.

SEED MIMIC
This ground-living tenebrionid beetle (*Helaeus subserratus*) from Western Australia hides from predators by looking like a seed.

Violin beetle

DUNG ROLLERS
Helped by her mate, this green scarab beetle is rolling her ball of buffalo dung to a burrow she has dug nearby. Here she will knead it before laying an egg in the center.

Brentid beetle

Head

Eye

Eye

Neck

Giraffe beetle

Wingless female lycid beetle

VIOLIN BEETLE
This beetle (*Mormolyce phyllodes*) is flat because it lives between the layers of bracket fungi on Indonesian trees.

European glowworm

LIGHT WORK
Glowworms are not worms, but beetles. The wingless females of some species can flash their tails to attract a mate.

LYCID BEETLE
This female beetle, (*Demosis* species) is called a "trilobite larva," because it looks like the now extinct sea-dwelling trilobites.

STICKING HIS NECK OUT
Only the male Madagascan giraffe beetle (*Tachelophorus giraffa*) has a long neck. In contrast, the front of the head of both the male and the female of this large Malaysian brentid (*Eutrachelus temmincki*) looks as though it has been stretched.

Flies

A FLY IS AN INSECT WITH TWO WINGS. Many other insects are called flies, like butterflies and dragonflies, but they have four wings and are not true flies. Instead of hind wings, flies have a pair of small drumstick-like structures called halteres, which are important for balancing in flight. Flies have large compound eyes (pp. 14–15) and claws and pads on the feet so they can walk on any surface. They can perform amazing acrobatics in the air, walking on the ceiling, flying backward, and hovering on the spot. True flies are found all over the world from the icy polar regions to the equatorial rain forest. Some kinds of flies help humans by pollinating crops, but many, like mosquitos, are dangerous pests. They spread diseases, such as malaria and sleeping sickness, and carry germs. All flies undergo complete metamorphosis (pp. 24–25). The grubs, or maggots, live mainly in water or in moist, rotting plant and animal tissue. A few species feed only on living plants or animals.

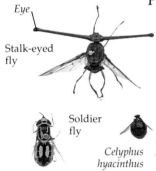

NO FLIES ON ME!
This character in the film *Return of the Fly* is gradually turning into a fly.

WINGLESS
This tiny bat fly (*Penicillidia fulvida*) has no wings at all. It lives in the fur of bats and feeds on blood. The female gives birth to a fully grown grub that falls to the ground and pupates (pp. 24–25).

European crane fly

Eye

Stalk-eyed fly

AN EYE FOR AN EYE
The stalked eyes of this male fly (*Achias rothschildi*) from New Guinea are used to threaten other males with shorter eye stalks. The fly with the longest eye stalks wins.

Soldier fly

Celyphus hyacinthus

BEETLE MIMIC
This small fly (*Celyphus hyacinthus*) from Malaysia looks remarkably like a beetle.

GREEN SKIN
The green color of this South American soldier fly (*Hedriodiscus pulcher*) is caused by an unusual green pigment in the cuticle (p. 6) rather than by iridescence (a trick of the light).

LONG-LEGGED CRANE FLIES
There are around 10,000 known species of crane fly in the world, and this species of *Holorusia*, from China, is one of the largest. The smaller species (*Ctenophora ornata*) is from Europe. Crane fly maggots have such a tough covering that they are often called "leatherjackets." They usually live in wet ground or muddy streams and feed on plant roots. Some species are pests on grass roots.

Halteres used for balancing

The world's biggest crane fly

FATTEST FLY
The grubs of this South American fly (*Pantophthalmus bellardii*) bore into living wood. Little is known about the habits of these large adults, and it may be that they do not even feed.

Dung fly

Housefly

DUNG FEEDERS
Dung flies, like this European species (*Scathophaga stercoraria*), are commonly seen on wet cow dung. Houseflies (*Musca domestica*) also breed on animal dung, as well as on decaying meat and vegetables. If food is left uncovered, houseflies will soon begin feeding, and in this way they spread many diseases.

NO EYE STALKS
This African fly (*Clitodoca fenestralis*) is related to the stalk-eyed fly from New Guinea shown above, but nothing is known about its life-style. The patterned wings and red head may be important in courtship.

FLESH EATERS
The female of this human warble fly (*Dermatobia hominis*) lays her eggs on a mosquito. When the mosquito feeds on a human, the eggs hatch and the fly larva begins to bore under the human's skin, where it lives and feeds for about six weeks. Like the housefly, bluebottles (*Cynomya mortuorum*) are common pests, breeding in rotting meat and dead bodies, and spreading disease.

Human warble fly

Bluebottle

OUT OF THE STRONG CAME FORTH SWEETNESS
According to the Old Testament, Samson saw a swarm of bees in the dead and rotting body of a lion. In fact, the insects he saw were almost certainly not bees, but yellow and black drone flies. These flies look like bees, but their larvae live and pupate in putrid water. This probably fooled ancient writers into believing that bees lived in the bodies of dead animals.

Long tongue for feeding on nectar

SPIDER EATER
The maggots of this fly (*Lasia corvina*) feed in live tarantula spiders.

FLAT FLOWER-FEEDER
This fly (*Trichophthalma philippii*) from Argentina sips nectar. The maggots feed in live scarab beetle grubs.

Short, biting mouthparts

FLY-FISHING
People who fish disguise their hooks with fantastic "flies" like this, made from feathers and twine. Floating on the surface, the mock fly fools fish into thinking it is a drowning insect.

A VARIED DIET
This horsefly (*Philoliche longirostris*) from Nepal has short, biting mouthparts to feed on blood, and a long tongue to sip nectar.

Long, beelike tongue for sipping nectar

TACHINID FLIES
There are many thousands of species of tachinid fly in the world. The maggots are always parasitic; that is, they feed on other insects while they are still alive. For this reason they are often important in controlling pests. The yellowish species (*Paradejeeria rutiloides*) is from America, where it attacks moth caterpillars. The brilliant green species (*Formosia moneta*) from New Guinea feeds on scarab beetle larvae.

MEAT-EATING MAGGOTS
This African bee fly (*Ligyra venus*) feeds on nectar, but its maggots eat developing grubs in wasps' nests.

A SLIM PROFILE
Like the true bees, this slender-bodied bee fly (a species of *Systropus*) from Java sips nectar. Its larvae feed on live moth caterpillars.

BEE-EATING BEE FLIES
This European bee fly (*Bombylius discolor*) is easily mistaken for a bumblebee feeding on nectar. Its maggots feed on grubs in the nests of solitary bees.

Syrphus torvus

Volucella zonaria

HOVER FLIES
The name of these flies refers to their amazing ability to hang in the air almost motionless, then dart away, almost too quick to be seen. Many of the species are striped yellow and black and look like wasps or bees. The maggots of the smaller species (*Syrphus torvus*) are popular with gardeners in Europe because they feed on aphids and keep numbers down. The maggots of *Volucella zonaria* scavenge for food beneath wasps' nests.

This robber fly (*Dioctria linearis*) is feeding on an ichneumon fly it has captured

Mallophora atra

Pagidolaphria flammipennis

Wing

Plumed legs may help this fly attract his mate

Leg

Blepharotes splendissimus

Pegesimallus teratodes

ROBBER FLIES
The members of this large family get their name from their habit of perching on suitable lookout points and attacking other insects flying past. They can be pests around beehives, killing bees as they fly home. The large black species (*Mallophora atra*) from South America probably mimics carpenter bees (p. 38). The remarkable male with plumed legs (*Pegesimallus teratodes*) is from Africa. It is thought that he waves his legs to try and attract a mate.

LARGEST FLY
This South American mydas fly (*Mydas heros*) is probably the largest in the world. The maggots live in ants' nests, feeding on beetles - which are themselves scavenging on the rubbish left by the ants.

Butterflies and moths

BUTTERFLIES AND MOTHS together form a single group of around 200,000 known species. It is sometimes difficult to tell a butterfly from a moth, but, generally, butterflies are brightly colored and fly during the day (or, rarely, early evening), whereas the more subtly colored moths are usually night-fliers. The antennae of most butterflies are clubbed, rather than straight or feathery, like moths' antennae, and butterflies rest with their wings folded upright over their backs, while moths hold them flat and roof-like over the body. Adult butterflies and moths feed on liquids, which they suck up through a long, coiled "proboscis." Their wings and body are covered in tiny scales, which are really flattened and ridged hairs. All species undergo complete metamorphosis (pp. 24–25), and the larvae, or caterpillars, are as varied in color and shape as the adults.

Jemadia hewitsonii

Hooked antenna

Amenis baroni

BUTTERFLY OR MOTH?
The skippers are like both butterflies and moths. Their antennae are thickened and hooked, rather than clubbed like those of true butterflies. Adults are usually brown – in contrast to these two brightly colored species from Peru.

NYMPHALID BUTTERFLY
The deep, intense blue of this nymphalid (*Asterope sapphira*) is caused by the way the light strikes the tiny scales that cover the wings.

GEOMETRID MOTHS
The caterpillars of geometrids are called inchworms. The adults of many species, like this night-flying great oak beauty from Europe (*Boarmia roboraria*), are camouflaged pale green or light brown. The bright colors of *Milionia weliskei* from Southeast Asia suggest that it is day-flying and not very tasty for birds.

Feathery antenna

DON'T EAT ME!
In insects a combination of red, yellow, and black is often an indication that an insect is poisonous. This day-flying zygaenid moth (*Campylotes desgodinsi*) from Southeast Asia is probably avoided by birds because of its colors.

SPECIAL LEGS
Some butterflies use their front pair of legs for cleaning their eyes, rather than for walking.

OLD LADY MOTH
This old lady moth (*Mormo maura*) from Europe flies at night. During the day its drab-colored wings conceal it on trees where it rests.

Feather-like moth antenna

Eyespot

END OF A TAIL
The eyespots on the wings of this African moon moth (*Argema mimosae*) probably divert predators away from the delicate body. Similarly, the long tails will break off if the moth is attacked. In the light the green color quickly fades. Zulus are said to have used the silvery cocoons of this African species as ankle decorations.

Sunset moth

URANIID MOTHS
The uraniid moths are found only in the tropics, where they are often confused with butterflies. Many, like the Madagascan sunset moth (*Chrysiridia ripheus*), are day-flying, and several have been known to migrate long distances. The brilliant iridescent colors on the wings are produced by scales that catch the light as it flies. The blue and white species (*Alcides aurora*) comes from New Guinea and has fanlike hind wings.

Alcides aurora

Hind wings look like fans

Long tails will break off if caught

BUTTERFLY WINGS
Butterflies rest with their wings folded together above their back.

Underside

Upper side

COME IN, NUMBER 89!
These two South American 89 butterflies (*Diaethria marchalii*) are identical – the left one shows the underside of the right one. A bird chasing the bright, blue spots on the wings will lose sight of them as soon as the butterfly settles and folds its wings.

Scent scales

PERFUME FOR THE LADY
This colorful South American butterfly (*Agrias claudina sardanapalus*) feeds on rotting fruit. The males have bright yellow scent scales on the inside of the hind wings, which help to attract the females.

Very few scales make wings clear

A SEE-THROUGH CHARACTER
Some butterflies and moths, like this South American species (*Cithaerias esmeralda*), have see-through wings, making them difficult targets for predators.

UNDER THREAT
The destruction of forests in Indonesia means this glass swallowtail (*Papilio karna carnatus*) may soon die out (p. 63).

PUPAE
When a caterpillar has eaten enough, it turns into a pupa. As soon as this splits open, the adult emerges.

CATERPILLARS
The eggs of butterflies and moths hatch into caterpillars.

Tail deflects predators' attention from head

SWALLOWTAIL BUTTERFLIES
The swallowtails, some of the most beautiful butterflies in the world, get their name from their peculiarly extended hind wings, which often look like the forked tail of a swallow. Because of its unusually clubbed hind wings, this common clubtail butterfly (*Pachliopta coon coon*) flies rather haphazardly and is often difficult to catch.

Male bird-wing butterfly

Abdomen

Female bird-wing butterfly

Metallic fleck

METALMARKS
These butterflies often have metallic flecks on their wings. The six tails of this species (*Helicopis cupido*) help confuse predators.

BETTER RED THAN DEAD
The deep red of this red glider butterfly (*Cymothoe coccinata*) is probably difficult to see in the colorful West African tropical forest where it lives. The underside is brown like a dead leaf.

BIRD-WING BUTTERFLIES
The name of this species, *Ornithoptera croesus*, refers to the golden colors of the male. The female is one of the largest butterflies in the world and spends most of her life high in the trees. The future of many bird-wing species is threatened because the forest in which they live is gradually being cut down (p. 63).

Bugs

THE WORD "BUG" is used loosely to describe any crawling insect. But bugs are a special group of insects with a long, jointed feeding tube specially adapted to piercing and sucking. Bugs include water boatmen and water striders (pp. 48–49), which suck the juices from other insects in ponds; plant-sucking aphids, scale insects, exotic seed bugs, and lantern flies; and bloodsucking bedbugs and assassin bugs, some of which spread dangerous diseases in humans. The front wings of many bugs are hard and horny at the base with thin, overlapping tips that cover and protect the delicate, membranous hind wings. Many plant-sucking bugs have entirely membranous front wings. All bugs undergo incomplete metamorphosis (pp. 26–29), and the little bugs look very similar to their parents, except that they are smaller and have no wings.

Curved rostrum

HISSING ASSASSIN
Assassin bugs, like this species (*Rhinocoris alluaudi*), can produce hissing sounds by rasping their curved feeding tube, or rostrum, against a filelike structure under the body.

WHO NEEDS MEN!
Many aphids, like the one shown above, bear live young and can reproduce by "parthenogenesis" – without males.

Locris adult

SPITTING WITH RAIN *above left*
This adult African froghopper (*Locris* species) produces so much froth in the big trees where it lives that the froth falls to the ground like rain.

IT'S FROTHY, MAN
The froth "cuckoo spit" is produced by young plant-feeding froghoppers to protect them from drying out and possibly from being eaten.

LEAFHOPPERS
This leafhopper (*Graphocephala fennahi*) feeds on rhododendron leaves. Other leafhopper species, usually green in color, damage the leaves of many plants including roses and cotton plants.

GROUND PEARLS
Many bugs are wingless and barely look like insects. These "ground pearls" are the hard skins of a group of bugs that feed on plant roots.

Ground pearls (*Margarodes formicarum*)

Bedbugs (enlarged)

Bedbug (natural size)

NIGHTTIME PESTS
The bedbug (*Cimex lectularis*) belongs to a small family of bloodsucking bugs, most of which live in the roosts and nests of bats and birds. They all feed on blood, and can survive without food for several months. They reproduce fastest in warm conditions, such as houses with warm bedrooms.

Eye

Strong, grasping front legs seize small water creatures

Ceratocoris horni

Spiny legs may be used for fighting

Thasus acutangulus

Spines may deter birds

Hemikyptha marginata

UNUSUAL PLANT FEEDERS
The reason for the strange shapes and variety of sizes of many plant-feeding bugs often remains a complete mystery. Some have unusual legs, like the spiny-legged bug on the left (*Thasus acutangulus*), and others have strange shapes (*Hemikyptha marginata*) or horns (*Ceratocoris horni*).

Scale insects (*Coccus hesperidum*)

Mealybugs (*Planococcus citri*)

SAP SUCKERS
Mealybugs, scale insects, and ground pearls are all bugs in which the wingless adult females have become little more than sap-sucking bags.

SERENADING CICADAS
Cicadas, like this Indian species (*Angamiana aetherea*), have been famous throughout history for the songs the males use to attract females. The nymphs (pp. 26–27) live underground, sucking sap from plant roots. In North America one species takes 17 years to become adult. Whole populations of adults emerge at the same time, crawl up trees, and sing for a few weeks.

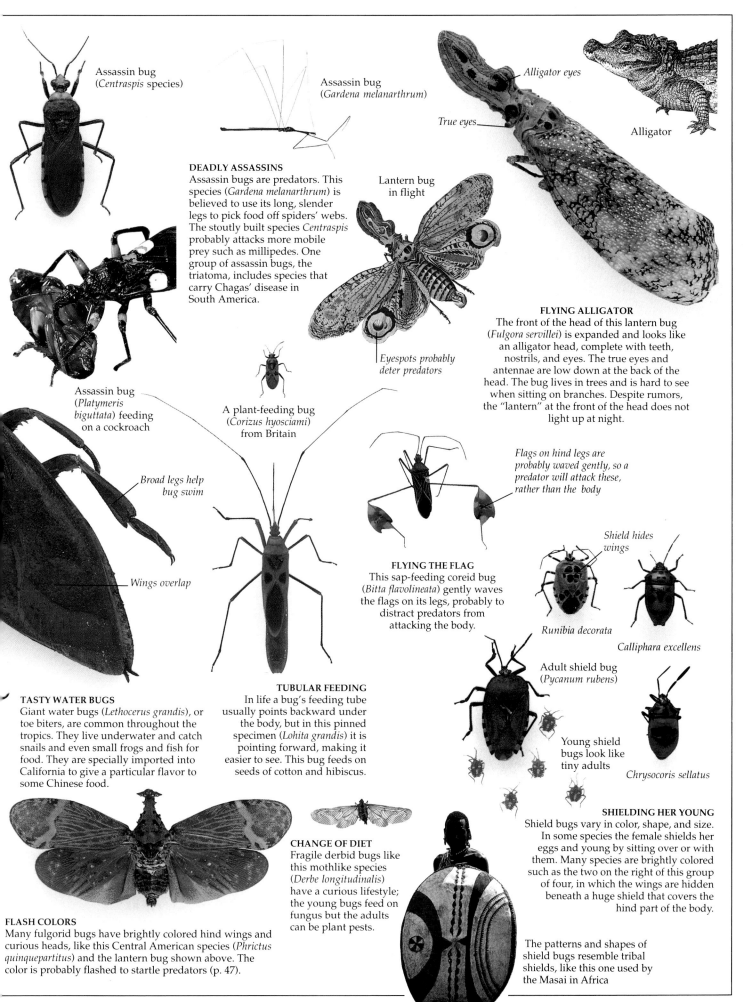

Assassin bug
(*Centraspis* species)

Assassin bug
(*Gardena melanarthrum*)

Alligator eyes

True eyes

Alligator

DEADLY ASSASSINS
Assassin bugs are predators. This species (*Gardena melanarthrum*) is believed to use its long, slender legs to pick food off spiders' webs. The stoutly built species *Centraspis* probably attacks more mobile prey such as millipedes. One group of assassin bugs, the triatoma, includes species that carry Chagas' disease in South America.

Lantern bug
in flight

Eyespots probably deter predators

FLYING ALLIGATOR
The front of the head of this lantern bug (*Fulgora servillei*) is expanded and looks like an alligator head, complete with teeth, nostrils, and eyes. The true eyes and antennae are low down at the back of the head. The bug lives in trees and is hard to see when sitting on branches. Despite rumors, the "lantern" at the front of the head does not light up at night.

Assassin bug
(*Platymeris biguttata*) feeding
on a cockroach

A plant-feeding bug
(*Corizus hyosciami*)
from Britain

Flags on hind legs are probably waved gently, so a predator will attack these, rather than the body

Broad legs help bug swim

Shield hides wings

Wings overlap

FLYING THE FLAG
This sap-feeding coreid bug (*Bitta flavolineata*) gently waves the flags on its legs, probably to distract predators from attacking the body.

Runibia decorata

Calliphara excellens

Adult shield bug
(*Pycanum rubens*)

TASTY WATER BUGS
Giant water bugs (*Lethocerus grandis*), or toe biters, are common throughout the tropics. They live underwater and catch snails and even small frogs and fish for food. They are specially imported into California to give a particular flavor to some Chinese food.

TUBULAR FEEDING
In life a bug's feeding tube usually points backward under the body, but in this pinned specimen (*Lohita grandis*) it is pointing forward, making it easier to see. This bug feeds on seeds of cotton and hibiscus.

Young shield bugs look like tiny adults

Chrysocoris sellatus

SHIELDING HER YOUNG
Shield bugs vary in color, shape, and size. In some species the female shields her eggs and young by sitting over or with them. Many species are brightly colored such as the two on the right of this group of four, in which the wings are hidden beneath a huge shield that covers the hind part of the body.

CHANGE OF DIET
Fragile derbid bugs like this mothlike species (*Derbe longitudinalis*) have a curious lifestyle; the young bugs feed on fungus but the adults can be plant pests.

FLASH COLORS
Many fulgorid bugs have brightly colored hind wings and curious heads, like this Central American species (*Phrictus quinquepartitus*) and the lantern bug shown above. The color is probably flashed to startle predators (p. 47).

The patterns and shapes of shield bugs resemble tribal shields, like this one used by the Masai in Africa

Wasps, bees, and ants

WASPS, BEES, ANTS, and their relatives comprise one of the largest groups of insects in the world. Today there are about 200,000 known species, but many more are constantly being discovered. Apart from the sawflies, all wasps, bees, and ants are easy to recognize by the narrow "waist." At the end of the abdomen of many female wasps and bees, the egg-laying apparatus, or ovipositor, is modified as a painful sting for use in self-defense (pp. 46–47). Several species of wasps, bees, and ants are "social" insects, meaning that many of them live together looking after their brood communally in a nest they build themselves (pp. 52–55). Since the earliest times, humans have kept bees for honey (pp. 58–59) and been fascinated by the complex societies of ants (pp. 56–57), but comparatively little is known of wasps, despite their importance to us. Many wasps spend their lives killing the grubs and caterpillars of insects that damage and destroy crops. Together with bees they are also important pollinators, ensuring that our fruit and vegetable crops flourish.

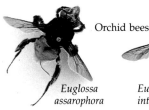

WASP WAIST
In the late 19th century tiny "wasp waists" were the height of female fashion.

Male

TREE WASPS
In summer tree wasp workers (*Dolichovespula sylvestris*) help farmers by killing caterpillars to feed their grubs. In autumn, when there are no more grubs to feed, they become household pests searching for sugary foods.

Queen

Worker

Sting injects poison into victim causing a painful wound

STING
This is a highly magnified photograph of a sting – a modification of the egg-laying apparatus of many bees and wasps.

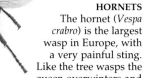

Hornet

HORNETS
The hornet (*Vespa crabro*) is the largest wasp in Europe, with a very painful sting. Like the tree wasps the queen overwinters and begins her nest in spring. Her first eggs hatch into female workers, which take over the tasks of expanding the nest and providing food for the grubs and for the queen herself, who goes into full-time egg production. Males are produced later along with the next season's queens.

SPIDER KILLERS
The tarantula hawk (*Pepsis heros*) is the world's largest wasp. The female wasp captures a large spider and paralyzes it with her sting. She then lays an egg on its motionless body, while it is still alive, and pushes it into a small burrow. When the egg hatches, the developing grub has a ready supply of fresh spider meat on which to feed.

Parasitic bee

PARASITIC BEE
Most bees are not social and do not build large nests like the honeybee (pp. 58–59). This large blue species (*Aglae caerulea*) is parasitic and lays its eggs in the cells made by orchid bees (below); the developing grub then eats the orchid bee grub as well as its food store.

Orchid bees

Euglossa assarophora

Euglossa intersecta

PERFUME MAKERS
Orchid bees from South America are so-called because the males visit orchid flowers, where they collect a substance that they then convert into a scent to attract females.

BIGGEST BEE
This Asian carpenter bee (*Xylocopa laticeps*) is the largest bee in the world. It makes nests in the tunnels it digs in rotting wood. The males often defend their territories by buzzing around intruders.

BUMBLEBEES
Like the honeybees, bumblebees are social insects and live in groups. They are found all in temperate areas all over the north. This mountain bumblebee (*Bombus monticola*) nests in a burrow in the ground, often close to bilberry bushes.

BORING INTO TREES
Female ichneumon wasps lay their eggs on other insects which the developing larvae consume. This female European rhyssa wasp (*Rhyssa persuasoria*) uses her extraordinarily long egg-laying apparatus, or ovipositor, to drill through wood to reach a live, wood-boring sawfly grub, on which she lays her egg. Particularly remarkable is this wasp's ability to locate the grub within the wood.

Long ovipositor

Male

Female has long abdomen for laying eggs

LONG ABDOMEN *left*
This female American wasp (*Pelecinus polyturator*) has a long, thin abdomen to reach into rotting wood and lay her eggs on beetle grubs. The male looks quite different.

Amblyteles wasp

Chrysalis

FUSSY FEEDERS
Many wasp species are quite specific about where they lay their eggs and where their grubs will feed. This European ichneumon wasp (*Amblyteles armatorius*) will only develop inside the chrysalis of one particular species of moth.

Cocoons of Apanteles *wasp*

PARASITIC WASPS
Many braconid wasps can develop inside a single caterpillar. The African species (*Apanteles gratiosus*) lays its eggs on hairy caterpillars. After the tiny grubs have eaten the inside of the caterpillar, they form cocoons on the surface.

CONSUMED FROM WITHIN
A new generation of parasitic wasps will soon emerge from the cocoons on this hawk moth caterpillar.

The larvae of this African wasp (*Chalinus imperialis*) feed on beetle grubs in wood

This giant wood wasp (*Urocerus gigas*), from Scandinavia, is a pest of pine trees

The grub of this species (*Cimbex femoratus*), from Europe, feeds on birch leaves

SAWFLIES
The sawflies differ from other wasps in not having a typical "wasp waist." They owe their name to the sawlike blades of the egg-laying apparatus, or ovipositor, which the females use to insert eggs into plant tissues. The grubs, which often look like moth caterpillars, feed on plants, sometimes forming galls or boring into stems. Unlike most other insect groups, sawflies are much less common in the tropics than in temperate parts of the world.

BUTTERFLY HUNTER
This handsome wasp (*Editha magnifica*) from South America attacks butterflies as they sit in groups on the ground. The wasp stings the butterflies one at a time, bites off their wings, and stores the bodies in a burrow in which it lays its eggs. The developing grubs feed on the butterflies' bodies until they are large enough to pupate.

Ants

Ants live in colonies in which there may be as many as 100,000 individuals (pp. 56–57). They have remarkably strong jaws and can give a painful nip. When some species bite, they are able to squirt formic acid from the end of their abdomen into the wound – making it doubly painful.

Driver ant winged male, or "sausage fly"

FLYING SAUSAGES
The winged male African driver ants are often called "sausage flies" because of their long, fat sausage-like bodies.

Dinoponera grandis

Driver ant workers

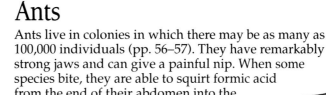

Driver ant queen

DRIVER ANTS
These African driver ants (*Dorylus nigricans*) form large colonies but they do not have permanent nests. They set up temporary camps, or bivouacs, while the queen lays eggs; then they move on, carrying with them the developing grubs. Periodically the ants fan out and eat everything in their path.

LARGEST ANT
Dinoponera ants from South America have the largest known workers. These live in small colonies but, unlike many ants, they are solitary hunters.

Ants communicate by touch and smell

HUNTING WASPS
This brilliant wasp (*Chlorion lobatum*) from India and Borneo catches and stings crickets in their burrows or on the soil surface. The wasp egg hatches, and the grub feeds on the cricket's body.

Other insects

JIMINY CRICKET
Walt Disney's Jiminy Cricket must be the only four-legged cricket in the world!

THERE ARE FIVE MAIN GROUPS of insects which we can all recognize: beetles, bugs, flies, wasps (including ants and bees), and butterflies and moths. These five include about three quarters of all insect species. However, there are at least another 15 similar but smaller groups. Several of these are shown here: cockroaches, earwigs, ant lions, dragonflies, mantises, grasshoppers, and stick insects. In addition to these groups of large insects there are also several groups of much smaller species. The most common are book lice, which live in packages of dried food; thrips, which can damage flowers; chewing lice, which live on birds; and fleas and sucking lice, which irritate people as well as animals.

STEPHENS ISLAND WETA
Except for on a few small islands, these large crickets, once common in New Zealand, are now almost extinct.

Stephens Island weta (*Deinacrida rugosa*)

Eurycantha calcarata from Papua New Guinea

Antenna

Slender, jointed leg

LIVING STICKS
Stick insects may be green or brown and are usually long and thin with slender legs and antennae. During the day they avoid attack by predators by hanging almost motionless in shrubs and trees where they look like just another twig (p. 45). At night they move around more and feed on leaves. The males of many species have wings; the females are often wingless.

Wing

Anchiole maculata from New Guinea

Grasping front legs make the insect look as though it is praying

Praying mantis (*Sibylla pretiosa*) from Africa

PRAYING FOR FOOD
Praying mantises are often slender, like stick insects. Many species are camouflaged in bright greens or dull browns (p. 45). They feed on other insects, which they grasp in their specially adapted front legs.

Strong hind legs enable fleas to jump great distances

Fleas

FLEAS
Adult fleas are bloodsuckers, each kind of flea preferring the blood of one kind of animal or bird. An animal flea will attack a human only if it is very hungry. The tiny white flea larvae do not feed on blood, but live on decaying material in nests and carpets. The adults can often survive without food for a long time, but as soon as a possible meal passes by, they quickly jump aboard.

Colors help conceal cricket on lichen-covered branches

Spines on legs protect against attack

SINGING TECHNIQUES
To attract females, male grasshoppers produce sounds by rubbing their hind legs against the hard front wings. This pale green African grasshopper (*Physemacris variolosa*) has a specially expanded abdomen to act as a resonating drum. In contrast crickets, like this Malaysian species (*Trachyzulpha fruhstorferi*), "sing" by rubbing the two front wings together (p. 12).

Grasshopper's expanded abdomen acts as a drum

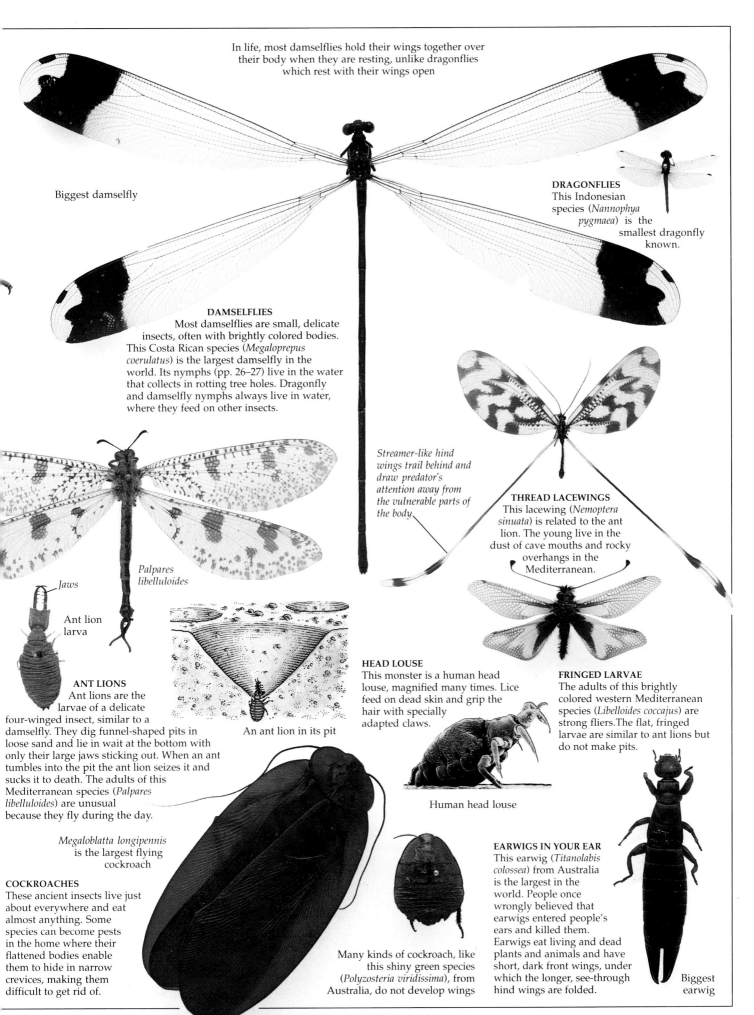

In life, most damselflies hold their wings together over their body when they are resting, unlike dragonflies which rest with their wings open

Biggest damselfly

DRAGONFLIES
This Indonesian species (*Nannophya pygmaea*) is the smallest dragonfly known.

DAMSELFLIES
Most damselflies are small, delicate insects, often with brightly colored bodies. This Costa Rican species (*Megaloprepus coerulatus*) is the largest damselfly in the world. Its nymphs (pp. 26–27) live in the water that collects in rotting tree holes. Dragonfly and damselfly nymphs always live in water, where they feed on other insects.

Streamer-like hind wings trail behind and draw predator's attention away from the vulnerable parts of the body.

THREAD LACEWINGS
This lacewing (*Nemoptera sinuata*) is related to the ant lion. The young live in the dust of cave mouths and rocky overhangs in the Mediterranean.

Jaws

Ant lion larva

Palpares libelluloides

ANT LIONS
Ant lions are the larvae of a delicate four-winged insect, similar to a damselfly. They dig funnel-shaped pits in loose sand and lie in wait at the bottom with only their large jaws sticking out. When an ant tumbles into the pit the ant lion seizes it and sucks it to death. The adults of this Mediterranean species (*Palpares libelluloides*) are unusual because they fly during the day.

An ant lion in its pit

HEAD LOUSE
This monster is a human head louse, magnified many times. Lice feed on dead skin and grip the hair with specially adapted claws.

FRINGED LARVAE
The adults of this brightly colored western Mediterranean species (*Libelloides coccajus*) are strong fliers.The flat, fringed larvae are similar to ant lions but do not make pits.

Human head louse

Megaloblatta longipennis is the largest flying cockroach

COCKROACHES
These ancient insects live just about everywhere and eat almost anything. Some species can become pests in the home where their flattened bodies enable them to hide in narrow crevices, making them difficult to get rid of.

EARWIGS IN YOUR EAR
This earwig (*Titanolabis colossea*) from Australia is the largest in the world. People once wrongly believed that earwigs entered people's ears and killed them. Earwigs eat living and dead plants and animals and have short, dark front wings, under which the longer, see-through hind wings are folded.

Many kinds of cockroach, like this shiny green species (*Polyzosteria viridissima*), from Australia, do not develop wings

Biggest earwig

Living with plants

IN THE COAL FORESTS that covered the Earth over 300 million years ago, there were very few kinds of insects. Dragonflies flew around the swampy areas (pp. 48–49), but butterflies, bugs, and beetles had scarcely evolved. Nor had the flowering plants and trees that are now so common throughout the world. The evolution of flowers and the increased variety of plants produced new opportunities that encouraged the evolution of many new species of insect. Some of these insects evolved as pollinators, others specialized in feeding on the rich food in buds and seeds; yet others fed on the many different types of leaves and fruit that gradually became available. The increase in the numbers of plant and insect species seems to have gone hand in hand. Equally important was the evolution of all the insects that live on dead plants and so restore nutrients to the soil – not to mention the wide range of predatory insects that feed on the plant eaters.

Female gall

Male galls

NAIL GALLS
In Australia, eucalyptus trees often produce galls when they are fed on by a group of unusual mealybugs (p. 36). This gall is short and round with four very long horns on top. When mature, the wingless female inside is fertilized by a winged male through a tiny hole between the horns. Males develop in nail-like galls that often grow on a female gall.

Beetle

Young adult beetle

LEAF MINERS
The pale, twisting trails on this leaf are caused by the tiny grubs of a species of small fly (*Phytomyza vitalbiae*). Each grub feeds on the living tissue between the upper and lower surface of the leaf. As it eats, it tunnels out its own shallow mine, leaving a trail of droppings behind it. These insects cause noticeable damage to green leaves and can eventually kill a healthy plant.

Beetle gall cut open

BEETLE GALL
These beetles (*Sagra femorata*) developed inside the swollen stem of a climbing plant. The swelling started when an adult female beetle laid her eggs in the stem. As the beetle grubs grew, so did the swelling, until the grubs were ready to metamorphose (pp. 23-24) into adults.

Tunnel caused by fly grub

FLOWERS
Many flowers rely on insects for pollination.

Black lines are the droppings that the grub produces as it eats its way along between the upper and lower surface of the leaf

1 A CLEAN BUMBLEBEE
Bees are essential to plants for carrying pollen from one flower to another, so ensuring that seeds are produced. For this reason, many flowers are brightly colored and scented in order to attract bees and other pollinating insects. The bumblebee, attracted by the sweet scent of the dog rose, lands to feed on pollen and sugary nectar.

Healthy green leaf attacked by leaf miners

2 DUSTED WITH GOLDEN POLLEN
As the bee sucks the nectar from the center of the dog rose using its long tongue, its hairy coat picks up grains of pollen from the stamens.

Pollen grains on stamens of flower

Yellow specks are pollen grains

YEW TREE GALLS
The tiny flies known as gall midges feed on many types of plant. On yew trees they cause the buds to stop growing and produce a ball of many small leaves. Each gall contains a single fly grub (*Taxomyia taxi*), and the small leaves turn brown as the fly matures.

Normal yew shoot

Yew gall

Yew gall

MARBLES ON OAK TREES
Oak marble galls are often common on oak trees in Europe. They are produced by the parthenogenetic females of a small gall wasp (*Andricus kollari*). The complete life-cycle, involving males and females, is still not fully understood.

Oak marble gall

CHERRIES ON OAK TREES
When a small gall wasp (*Cynips quercusfolii*) lays an egg in the vein of an oak leaf, a cherry gall is formed. Each gall grows around the developing grub, supplying it with food and protection.

Young gall is white

ROSE GALLS
Rose galls, or bedeguars (meaning "wind rose"), are caused when a tiny gall wasp (*Diplolepis rosae*) lays her eggs on rosebuds in spring. Each gall contains many wasp grubs in separate chambers.

PISTACHIO GALLS
These tubular galls are produced by pistachio trees around colonies of a particular aphid (*Baizongia pistaciae*) in the Mediterranean region. Like many other aphids, this species has two separate life-cycles, each on different plants.

Pistachio gall

Leaf

WIND ROSES
Hundreds of years ago in Persia, where modern roses came from, people believed that these pinkish, mosslike galls came on the wind and called them "wind roses."

Gall

Grub inside gall

Cherry galls on oak leaf

Young grub

Mature grub

Currant gall cut in half

CHERRY GALL
Only female gall wasps (*Cynips quercusfolii*) are produced in cherry galls. In winter these females lay eggs on oak tree buds, and in spring the grubs from these eggs give rise to males and females. These mate, and the females lay eggs on oak tree leaves to produce cherry galls again.

Silk strands

3 FILL YOUR BASKETS
As the bumblebee collects more and more pollen grains, it combs them from its body, packs them into the hairy pollen baskets on its hind legs, and then flies off to its nest. In domesticated honeybees (pp. 58–59), this pollen and nectar is stored in the hive as honey.

SAFE AND SOUND
Some caterpillars roll up a leaf, fix it with silk, then pupate safely hidden inside.

OAK CURRANTS
Female gall wasps (*Neuroterus quercusbaccarum*) lay eggs on oak tree catkins in spring, to produce a currant gall around each single wasp grub. These quickly develop to produce adult males and females. In summer, after mating, the females lay eggs on oak leaves. The oak tree produces a small, flat, reddish cushion called a spangle gall around each developing egg. The spangle gall falls to the ground, and in spring females emerge from this to lay eggs that develop parthenogenetically (p. 36).

Pollen packed into tiny baskets on hind legs

OAK APPLES
Oak apple galls are produced when a wingless female gall wasp (*Biorhiza pallida*) lays her eggs on an oak leaf bud. The group of small gall wasp grubs that develop by parthenogenesis (p. 36) give rise to winged males and females, in separate galls; these mate and the females lay eggs on the roots of the trees. Females produced on the roots are wingless and have to climb all the way up the oak trees to lay their eggs on the buds and so produce next year's oak apples.

Oak apple

Hide-and-seek

LEAF ME ALONE!
Some stick insects protect themselves against predators by looking like leaves. The wings are leaflike, and the legs have flattened plates along them to break up their outline.

Flatid bug on bark

Insects are eaten by many other animals. Without them, bats would not be able to live, and half the species of birds in the world would probably starve. Frogs, lizards, and alligators include insects in their diet, as do shrews, foxes, and monkeys. Many insects themselves hunt and kill other insects for food, and in some parts of the world even people eat insects. With this range of predators it is not surprising that many insect species have developed unusual colors, patterns, and shapes as ways of pretending they are something they are not. Some insects have oddly patterned or mottled wings to match the color of the bark on which they live. Other insects, like the leaf and stick insects, are so well disguised as leaves and twigs that they are ignored by would-be predators. Birds and lizards see such a protectively colored insect not as an insect but as the leaf it is imitating and leave it alone.

Flatid bug

BARK BUGS
Although there are many hundreds of species of flatid bug in the tropics, surprisingly little is known about the lifestyle of any of them. This Central American species (*Flatoides dealbatus*) apparently sits on the bark of trees, where its light brown coloring makes it difficult to see. Some species are see-through, or translucent, and others have mottled brown and gray patches to conceal them on lichen-covered trees where they rest.

CLICK BEETLE ON BARK
The whitish patches on the body of this click beetle (*Alaus* species) help it blend in with the patch of lichen on the bark of the tree where it was photographed in Nigeria (West Africa).

PLAYING DEAD
Old leaves often remain attached to trees and bushes long after they have dried to a crisp brown. This bush cricket (*Ommatoptera pictifolia*) from Brazil takes advantage of this by standing quite still on a twig. Even the most bright-eyed predator would be fooled into thinking it was a dead leaf – it even seems to have leaf veins.

Antennae held flat against bark

Veins on wings look like veins on a leaf

Sword-like egg-laying apparatus, or ovipositor

Legs hold body in a leaflike position

Slightly tattered wings break insect-like outline and make it look even more like an old dead leaf

Wings blend in with bark

BARK MIMIC
When it sits pressed closely against a small branch, this grayish-brown bush cricket (*Sathrophyllia rugosa*) from India looks just like a piece of bark. The wings of the insect merge with the roughness of the bark, and the cricket completely vanishes.

BREAK UP THE BORDERS
An important aspect of camouflage is to disrupt the outline of a familiar object so that it is more difficult to see. Many insects, like this mantid (*Gongylus gongylodes*), have flattened plates on their body and legs which probably help camouflage them in this way.

44

Lichen is a kind of plant that grows on tree trunks and on twigs

Mottled gray and white patches break outline of insect

Beetle

Lichen

Bark

LICHEN LONGHORNS

Longhorn beetles often mimic their surroundings or other insects (p. 46). This Madagascan species (*Lithinus nigrocristatus*) is remarkable for its ability to hide on lichen-covered twigs. It is almost impossible to see the four beetles hidden above.

Moth's folded wings are the same color as the lichen on the bark

Merveille du jour moth out of camouflage

Beetle

Beetle

Beetle

MERVEILLE DU JOUR MOTH

Many night-flying moths that spend their days resting on bark are well camouflaged against birds and lizards. Like the lichen longhorns, this merveille du jour moth (*Dichonia aprilina*) disappears from view in its natural habitat of lichen-covered trees. Out of camouflage it is much easier to spot.

CAMOUFLAGED STICKS

Live stick insects can be easy to overlook because when sitting quite still on leaves and twigs they are almost invisible. Occasionally some stick and leaf insects will gently sway from side to side, so all a predator sees is just another leaf or twig caught by the breeze. Even the eggs produced by female stick insects are similar in appearance to plant seeds.

Winged male of Macleay's specter (Extatosoma tiaratum) from Australia

Spiny green nymph (Eurycantha calcarata) (p. 40) from Papua New Guinea

Adult female green Indian stick insect (Carausius morosus)

Short-winged female of Macleay's specter (Extatosoma tiaratum)

Green, sticklike legs

Adult female pink-winged stick insect (Sipyloidea sipylus) from Indonesia

How to avoid being eaten

AVOIDING BEING EATEN by other animals is the key to survival for many insect species. Some insects do this by camouflage, blending in perfectly with their surroundings (pp. 44–45). Others have developed different ways of protecting themselves from their many enemies. After a nasty experience, hungry predators soon learn to leave poisonous or unpleasant-tasting insects alone, and will keep well out of the way of anything they know can give them a painful sting or bite. Some quite harmless insects take advantage of this by looking and behaving like poisonous or stinging creatures so that predators will mistake them for the real thing and will not even attempt to eat them. In some cases this mimicry is so good that it is difficult to see which insect is mimicking which. Other insects protect themselves in different ways – with clearly visible spines; bright, flashing colors to shock and surprise; strong, biting jaws; and powerful, kicking legs.

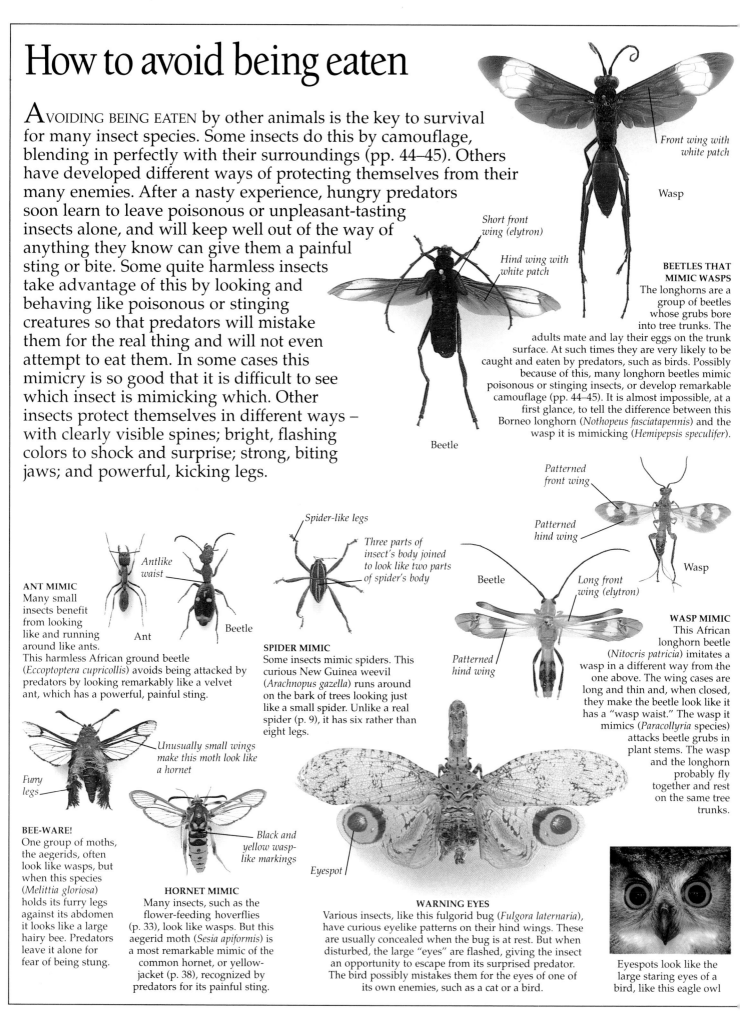

Front wing with white patch

Wasp

Short front wing (elytron)

Hind wing with white patch

Beetle

BEETLES THAT MIMIC WASPS

The longhorns are a group of beetles whose grubs bore into tree trunks. The adults mate and lay their eggs on the trunk surface. At such times they are very likely to be caught and eaten by predators, such as birds. Possibly because of this, many longhorn beetles mimic poisonous or stinging insects, or develop remarkable camouflage (pp. 44–45). It is almost impossible, at a first glance, to tell the difference between this Borneo longhorn (*Nothopeus fasciatapennis*) and the wasp it is mimicking (*Hemipepsis speculifer*).

Patterned front wing

Patterned hind wing

Wasp

Beetle

Spider-like legs

Three parts of insect's body joined to look like two parts of spider's body

Long front wing (elytron)

Patterned hind wing

ANT MIMIC

Many small insects benefit from looking like and running around like ants. This harmless African ground beetle (*Eccoptoptera cupricollis*) avoids being attacked by predators by looking remarkably like a velvet ant, which has a powerful, painful sting.

Antlike waist

Ant

Beetle

SPIDER MIMIC

Some insects mimic spiders. This curious New Guinea weevil (*Arachnopus gazella*) runs around on the bark of trees looking just like a small spider. Unlike a real spider (p. 9), it has six rather than eight legs.

WASP MIMIC

This African longhorn beetle (*Nitocris patricia*) imitates a wasp in a different way from the one above. The wing cases are long and thin and, when closed, they make the beetle look like it has a "wasp waist." The wasp it mimics (*Paracollyria* species) attacks beetle grubs in plant stems. The wasp and the longhorn probably fly together and rest on the same tree trunks.

Unusually small wings make this moth look like a hornet

Furry legs

BEE-WARE!

One group of moths, the aegerids, often look like wasps, but when this species (*Melittia gloriosa*) holds its furry legs against its abdomen it looks like a large hairy bee. Predators leave it alone for fear of being stung.

Black and yellow wasp-like markings

HORNET MIMIC

Many insects, such as the flower-feeding hoverflies (p. 33), look like wasps. But this aegerid moth (*Sesia apiformis*) is a most remarkable mimic of the common hornet, or yellow-jacket (p. 38), recognized by predators for its painful sting.

Eyespot

WARNING EYES

Various insects, like this fulgorid bug (*Fulgora laternaria*), have curious eyelike patterns on their hind wings. These are usually concealed when the bug is at rest. But when disturbed, the large "eyes" are flashed, giving the insect an opportunity to escape from its surprised predator. The bird possibly mistakes them for the eyes of one of its own enemies, such as a cat or a bird.

Eyespots look like the large staring eyes of a bird, like this eagle owl

CHEMICAL GUN
When a bombardier beetle (*Brachinus crepitans*) is disturbed, it can mix two harmless chemicals at the tip of its abdomen to produce a sudden explosion that frightens away predators.

Small postman butterfly (*Heliconius erato*) from southern Ecuador

SNAKE IN THE GRASS
Rather than mimicking insects, some caterpillars have unusually large heads to trick predators into thinking they are small but very poisonous snakes. When alarmed, this hawkmoth caterpillar (*Leucorhampha ornatus*) from Brazil rears its head and inflates its thorax to look like a snake's head.

False snake eye

Inflated thorax

Small postman butterfly (*Heliconius erato*) from western Brazil

RINGS OF MIMICS
Some groups of butterflies, such as the heliconiids, feed, particularly as larvae, on rather poisonous plants. As a result the adult butterflies often taste unpleasant and are avoided by insect-eating birds. Different species may take advantage of this by mimicking each other's color patterns. These species may also vary in color from place to place. These six butterflies represent two species from three different parts of South America.

Small postman butterfly (*Heliconius erato*) from southern Brazil

Postman butterfly (*Heliconius melpomene*) from western Brazil

Postman butterfly (*Heliconius melpomene*) from southern Brazil

Postman butterfly (*Heliconius melpomene*) from southern Ecuador

Long, slender antenna

Spiny hind legs raised to frighten or injure predator

Egg-laying apparatus, or ovipositor

FEEDING, NOT FIGHTING
The formidable spines and large jaws shown in this engraving of a South American cricket are for holding and eating prey – but they would also deter predators.

Spiny hind legs

1 WARNING WETA
Because the wildlife in New Zealand developed without any mammals, one group of large crickets called weta (p. 40) filled the role of the ground-living predators, eating a diet similar to that of shrews. These enormous insects are now almost extinct except on small islands, since humans introduced rats into their habitat.

2 STICK 'EM UP!
When disturbed, this species (*Hemideina thoracica*) raises its hind legs into a threatening posture. The spines on the legs can cause a nasty wound when the insect kicks.

A watery life

Mayfly adult

INSECTS EVOLVED ON LAND. This is clear from their breathing system (pp. 6–7), which takes in air from the atmosphere. Water insects have therefore had to adapt and must either swim to the surface for air, or develop ways of extracting air from the water, like fish. Some insects, such as dragonflies and many true flies, take advantage of the food supplies in water for their feeding and growing phase – the larva or nymph – and become winged and independent of water in the adult phase. Other insects have adapted wholly to water and spend their entire life cycle there. The adults leave the water only when they need to fly to new areas.

SKATING
Pond skaters (*Gerris lacustris*) skim over the surface, feeding on drowning insects.

Prey is held in four front legs

Oarlike hind legs

Sucking mouthparts

Eye

Silvery film of air around body

Hairs help bug swim

Pincer-like legs

SURFACE HUNTERS
Water boatmen (*Notonecta glauca*) are predatory bugs that swim upside down just beneath the surface, attacking and eating other insects that have fallen in. Water boatmen come to the surface to breathe. They push the tip of their abdomen above the surface, and store air under their wings, from where it can gradually be taken in through the spiracles (p. 7).

SWIMMING SAUCERS
Saucer bugs (*Ilyocoris cimicoides*) have strong front legs for grasping their prey and can give a painful "bite" if handled.

Strong pincer-like front legs

SAUCER BUG
The silvery underside of a saucer bug is caused by a film of air, or plastron, trapped beneath tiny hairs. Oxygen diffuses directly into the plastron from the water.

GIANT WATER BUG
This giant water bug, shown smaller than life size, was drawn by Maria Merian (1700) in Surinam.

Air is stored beneath the wings

Fringes on legs propel beetle through water

Gills extract oxygen from water

PREDATORY DAMSEL
Damselfly nymphs (p. 26) breathe by means of three external gills at the tip of the abdomen.

DIVING BEETLES
The great diving beetles (*Dytiscus marginalis*) are fierce predators of small fish and insects. They store air under their wings, like water boatmen, and occasionally fly from one pond to another.

Segmented antenna

Strong, grasping front legs

Sucker-like pads used in mating

CADDIS FLY LARVAE
The larvae of many caddis flies (*Limnephilus* species) spin a tube of silk onto which they stick small stones, sand, or pieces of plant to act as camouflage and protection.

Pieces of plant

Caddis fly larvae

Sticks and stones

WATER BEETLE PUPA
The larva of the great diving beetle crawls out of the pond and burrows into damp soil, where it pupates (pp. 24–25). After emerging, the young adult stays in the pupal cell for a few hours while the wing cases harden.

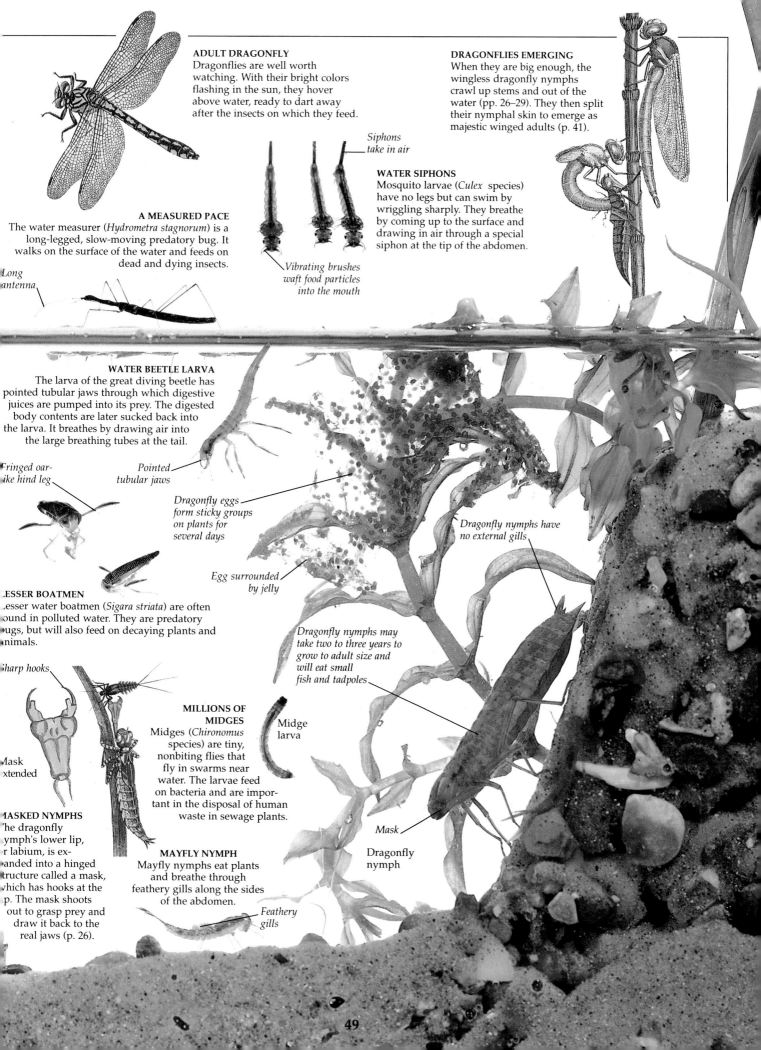

ADULT DRAGONFLY
Dragonflies are well worth watching. With their bright colors flashing in the sun, they hover above water, ready to dart away after the insects on which they feed.

DRAGONFLIES EMERGING
When they are big enough, the wingless dragonfly nymphs crawl up stems and out of the water (pp. 26–29). They then split their nymphal skin to emerge as majestic winged adults (p. 41).

Siphons take in air

WATER SIPHONS
Mosquito larvae (*Culex* species) have no legs but can swim by wriggling sharply. They breathe by coming up to the surface and drawing in air through a special siphon at the tip of the abdomen.

A MEASURED PACE
The water measurer (*Hydrometra stagnorum*) is a long-legged, slow-moving predatory bug. It walks on the surface of the water and feeds on dead and dying insects.

Long antenna

Vibrating brushes waft food particles into the mouth

WATER BEETLE LARVA
The larva of the great diving beetle has pointed tubular jaws through which digestive juices are pumped into its prey. The digested body contents are later sucked back into the larva. It breathes by drawing air into the large breathing tubes at the tail.

Fringed oar-like hind leg

Pointed tubular jaws

Dragonfly eggs form sticky groups on plants for several days

Dragonfly nymphs have no external gills

Egg surrounded by jelly

LESSER BOATMEN
Lesser water boatmen (*Sigara striata*) are often found in polluted water. They are predatory bugs, but will also feed on decaying plants and animals.

Dragonfly nymphs may take two to three years to grow to adult size and will eat small fish and tadpoles

Sharp hooks

MILLIONS OF MIDGES
Midges (*Chironomus* species) are tiny, nonbiting flies that fly in swarms near water. The larvae feed on bacteria and are important in the disposal of human waste in sewage plants.

Midge larva

Mask extended

MASKED NYMPHS
The dragonfly nymph's lower lip, or labium, is expanded into a hinged structure called a mask, which has hooks at the tip. The mask shoots out to grasp prey and draw it back to the real jaws (p. 26).

Mask

Dragonfly nymph

MAYFLY NYMPH
Mayfly nymphs eat plants and breathe through feathery gills along the sides of the abdomen.

Feathery gills

Building a nest

THE NESTS built by the common wasp (*Vespula vulgaris*) are always begun by a single queen working on her own. She builds a series of papery envelopes from chewed-up wood fibers and lays her eggs inside. She must safely rear her first batch of eggs through to adults. These then become the first workers who expand the nest and forage for food, so that the queen can remain within the nest laying more eggs. New nests are always built again each spring, except in parts of New Zealand where winters are mild enough for introduced European wasps to maintain their nests for several years.

THE START
The common wasp queen (*Vespula vulgaris*) starts a nest by building a short stalk with a cap, covering a comb of four or five cells. She lays one egg at the bottom of each cell.

Stalk attached to support

New envelope is built down and around older envelopes

1 INSULATING LAYERS
The queen builds a series of envelopes around her small comb. These layers insulate the developing larvae from cold winds. The nests of the common wasp are always built with the entrance at the bottom, unlike some tropical wasps' nests (pp. 52–54).

The queen lays one egg at the bottom of each paper cell

CARING FOR THE EGGS
When the eggs hatch, the queen must collect caterpillars as food for the developing grubs. She must also collect more material to extend the walls of the nest.

3 KEEPING GUARD
The nest entrance is now just a small hole. This is easier to defend from other insects, including other queens who might try to take over the nest. Keeping the hole small also makes it easier to control the temperature and humidity around the developing grubs.

Developing grub

2 THE WHITE HOUSE
This queen has found a source of nesting material which is almost white. She will visit this, between feeding her grubs, and chew away some wood fibers to make the "paper" from which she builds the nest.

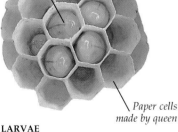

Paper cells made by queen

LARVAE
On their rich diet of chewed insects and caterpillars, the grubs are growing fast, each in its own cell. The time from egg to adult varies with the temperature and the amount of food available, but it is usually about five weeks.

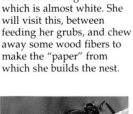

BUILDING WALLS
As the queen builds the nest she uses her antennae to measure the size of the envelopes and the cells.

White paper envelopes are made from fibers of wood which the queen chews and mixes with saliva to make a sort of "paper"

Entrance to nest is small to protect the larvae inside, and to help control the temperature and humidity

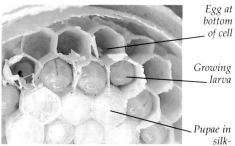

Egg at bottom of cell

Growing larva

Pupae in silk-capped cells

GRUBS WITH CAPS ON
When the larvae are fully grown, just before they pupate, they spin their own silken cap to close their cell. A few days later the first set of workers emerges and the nest can start to grow.

4 THE NEST CHANGES COLOR
The first workers produced in a nest are often very small. They immediately start to collect wood fibers from many different sources, and so the "paper" they make is often multicolored and striped. Wasps can often be seen on fence posts, scraping the surface in a series of parallel lines. Inside the nest the old paper envelopes are chewed away to make room for larger combs of cells.

5 HOW MANY WASPS?
A large nest of common wasps may measure as much as 18 in (45 cm) in diameter and may contain more than 500 adults in summer. Between spring and autumn it will produce several thousand individuals, most of whom die from exhaustion. Fresh eggs are laid in the cells of each comb as soon as they become vacant.

CROSS-SECTION
This old engraving, although stylized, shows how the envelopes surround the comb of cells in a young nest. Older nests will have four or five horizontal combs.

Darker speckles on walls may be the result of some of the workers having fed on poisonous, treated wood

The workers scrape fibers from many different types of wood, making the paper multicolored

UNDERGROUND NESTS
The common wasp often builds nests underground. As the nest grows the workers have to dig soil and stones away to provide more room. Sometimes small piles of stones can be found near the entrance to the nest.

6 THE NEXT GENERATION
In summer, the wasps construct several cells which are larger than normal. The grubs developing in these cells are given extra food. These larger grubs develop into males and queens, which fly from the nest and mate. The fertilized queens then find a quiet place to overwinter before starting a new nest the following spring.

Insect architects

WASPS, BEES, ANTS, AND TERMITES build a wide range of nests to protect their young. The simplest nest is a burrow in the soil made by a solitary wasp. The most complex is made by termites and contains millions of workers and a single queen. Some nests, like the ones built by common wasps (pp. 50–51), are started by a single queen and cannot grow until her first eggs hatch into adult workers. Others, like the honeybees' nest (pp. 58–59), are also started by a single queen, but she is aided by a swarm of female workers from an older nest. In South America, wasps' nests vary even more and may be started by single females, groups of cooperating females, or by swarms of females, sometimes with several queens.

LONG AND THIN
Ropalidia wasps, which are found from Africa to Australia, build simple, open nests. Each consists of only a few cells hanging from a central stalk. The female lays a single egg in each cell and feeds the grubs as they develop.

Leaf

Vertical combs

JOB SHARING
African *Belanogaster* wasps build exposed combs with long cells. Each nest is started by one female who is joined later by several others. Unlike many wasps these females do not have specific roles, though one female may lay most of the eggs.

LEAFY NEST
This common South American wasp species (*Protopolybia sedula*) builds a nest of up to ten vertical combs between the leaves of a plant. A large nest may contain up to 10,000 wasps.

MUD VASE
Oriental *Stenogaster* wasps produce attractive, vaselike nests of mud or mud and plant fibers. Each nest is made by a solitary female. She feeds her two or three grubs as they grow, then seals them up to pupate.

CLAY NEST
Unlike most large nests, which are made of plant fibers to keep them light, the nest of *Polybia singularis* is built largely of mud. Because each nest is so heavy, it must be hung from a stout branch.

Hole where branch went

OPEN HOUSE
These open nests are built in warm countries by *Polistes* wasps. Other wasps sometimes occupy the exposed combs, and drive the original builders away.

Walls are made largely of hardened mud, which the workers pick up wet from the sides of streams

Vertical slitlike entry hole is unique to this species of wasp

PAPER CONES

Nests built by the South American wasp *Chartergus globiventris* are collected frequently but have rarely been studied in their natural state. The cylindrical nests hang from a branch and always have a small entry hole at the bottom. They vary in size from about 2 in (5 cm) long and 1.2 in (3 cm) wide to 3 ft (100 cm) long and 6 in (15 cm) wide. The largest nests contain many thousands of wasps with several egg-laying queens. The size of the nest is thought to depend on the size of the swarm that begins building it, but much still remains to be discovered about these wasps.

Branch supporting nest

SPINY NEST

Polybia scutellaris is a common wasp in Argentina and southern Brazil, where nests are sometimes built under the eaves of houses. Each nest is made of chewed plant fibers, and the outer envelope is covered with hard papery spines.

Entrance hole

Papier-mâché walls made of plant fibers, which the adult wasps collect and chew into a paste

Hole at the center of each level allows wasps to move from floor to floor

Nest is made of chewed plant fibers

Papery spines

Entrance hole

CROSS-SECTION OF A CARTON NEST

This nest is similar to the one above, but it has been cut in half to show the inside. Each nest is built from plant fibers, which the adult wasps collect and chew into a paste like papier-mâché. They build several layers of combs for rearing their young, with a hole at the center of each layer, so they can easily move from floor to floor. The new combs are probably added at the bottom and then covered by a new envelope.

TREE HOUSES

This engraving shows another spiky nest. The entrance is different from the *Polybia scutellaris* nest above, suggesting that it may have been built by a different species.

Continued on next page

Nest of *Polybia scutellaris* from
South America

HOME PROTECTION

These wasps (*Apoica pallida*) build a simple, open nest with one comb of cells. The upper surface is protected by a conelike outer envelope made from plant fibers. In its natural state, the lower surface is protected by neat rows of wasps, all facing outward to ward off predators with an array of eyes and antennae – and the ever-ready stings.

Brood cells containing developing grubs

Spiny outer casing is made of chewed plant fibers

Entrance to nest

DRUMMERS' HOME

This simple nest with a single comb is built flat against a tree branch and enclosed in a ridged envelope made from chewed plant fibers. It is produced by a swarm of wasps that is thought to include several queens. These metallic blue wasps (*Synoeca surinama*) are among the largest social wasps in South America, with a powerful and painful sting. They fly quietly, but when annoyed they drum on the inside of their nest, producing a warning sound.

WINTER PROTECTION

Some *Polybia scutellaris* nests have been known to exist for 30 years, and the thick, spiny envelope may be important in protecting the wasps through the cooler winters of southern South America.

Mouthlike entrance

Termites

The biggest and most complex of insect societies are built by termites. The nests of some species, such as the West African *Macrotermes bellicosus* (below), may house up to five million – many more termites than the entire human population of New Zealand – and are extraordinarily complex buildings, with full air conditioning. Nests usually have a single queen, who lays all the eggs, and a single king, who fertilizes them all. In a really big nest a queen and king may live for 15 years, and for much of her life the queen will lay one egg every three seconds. She looks like a small sausage and lives in a special chamber; she is fed continuously by the numerous workers of her nest. Radiating out from the nest are many covered trails, guarded by large soldier termites, along which the workers bring all the food needed for the colony. Unlike ants, these soldiers and workers are male or female, and they all feed only on plant material. Some species attack young plants, others eat seeds, but most eat rotting wood or cultivate special fungus gardens.

TREE TERMITES
Many termite species build nests in trees; the nests are usually connected to other parts of the same colony, either underground or in other trees. Termites connect the galleries by sticking soil particles together and roofing in their highways, or by tunneling in wood and underground. The foraging galleries and tunnels of the *Macrotermes* nest shown on the right cover 2.5 acres (1 hectare).

AIR-CONDITIONED CITY
This towering mound built by West African termites (*Macrotermes bellicosus*) is really a giant ventilation chimney through which hot air from the nest can escape. Beneath the tower is a cave about 9 ft (3 m) in diameter housing the nursery galleries, the queen's cell, and the fungus gardens. Below the main cave are cavities 32 ft (10 m) or more deep, from which the termites obtain water. At the top of the main cave is a hole, which the termites can make bigger or smaller by adding or removing soil particles. This varies the speed of warm, moist air passing up and out through the cave and chimneys, and controls the temperature in the nest to within 1 degree.

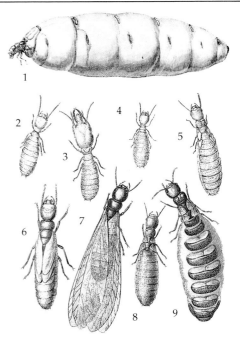

TERMITE CASTES
1) Fully grown *Macrotermes* queen; the head and thorax are dwarfed by the enormous abdomen; 2) worker; 3) soldier; 4) young nymph; 5) short-winged nymph; 6) long-winged nymph; 7) male; 8) young female; 9) egg-laying female (note wings cut off after mating flight).

Air escapes

Fungus gardens are cultivated for food

Queen cell, where eggs are produced

Air enters

Foraging tunnel

Nursery galleries, where larvae are tended

INSIDE A TERMITES' NEST
The *Macrotermes subhyalinus* nest differs from that of its relative *M. bellicosus*, but the principle of keeping a constant temperature within remains the same.

MYSTERIOUS UMBRELLAS
The study of insects often raises more questions than answers. These umbrella nests of African *Cubitermes* are well known. They are about 18 in (45 cm) high. But what is their function? A nest starts hidden underground. Then one or more columns may suddenly be built, and up to five caps may be added to each one. No queen cell is built by these termites.

Walls are made from tiny pellets of earth cemented together with saliva

Social ants

Ants are social insects, closely related to wasps and bees (pp. 38-39). Most ant species live and work together in big colonies, often building complex nests in which to rear their young. Each nest is begun by a single queen who lays all the eggs. There is no king; soon after she emerges from her pupa in the old nest, the young winged queen mates once with a winged male and stores the sperm to use throughout her life. She then bites off her wings and starts a new nest. The nest is built by wingless, sterile female workers, which forage for food and tend the developing eggs and grubs. Ant species vary greatly. There are solitary and parasitic species; ants that rear workers from other nests as slaves; and "cuckoo" queens that enter nests and persuade the workers to kill their queen so they can raise her brood.

ANTEATERS
Anteaters feed on ants and have powerful claws to break open nests and termite mounds and a long snout to reach inside.

WEIGHTLIFTERS
Tiny ants can lift objects that weigh more than they do. When a nest is disturbed, the ants rush about to defend and rebuild it; but their first priority is to move the brood to a place of safety deeper in the nest. The large white objects in this photograph are not eggs, but pupae, each with an almost mature adult inside.

WOOD ANTS
In forests wood ants are important insect predators and a large colony will collect many thousands of insects in one day. A large nest may contain 100,000 ants with several queens and can last for many years. In 1880 in Aachen, West Germany, the European wood ant became the first insect to be protected by a conservation law.

The leaves are carried right inside the nest where they are cut into small pieces and used as a basis for growing a kind of fungus on which the ants feed

The ants in the nest cut the leaves into smaller pieces and fertilize the fungal gardens with their excreta

The fungus flourishes only if attended by the ants – if neglected it will quickly die

Pieces of leaf are left at the entrance to the nest for the gardener ants, who pick them up and drag them inside

Parasol ants

The "parasols" of this trail of tropical American leaf-cutting ants (*Atta cephalotes*) are pieces of leaves and flowers, which each ant cuts out and carries back to the nest. In the nest they are cut into smaller pieces and used to grow a kind of fungus on which the ants feed. The nest is usually underground, and has special air conditioning to insure that the temperature and humidity remain almost constant. A large nest may be several yards across and will house a number of fungus gardens and separate brood chambers. A colony of parasol ants consumes a vast quantity of leaves. In their natural habitat, where they are part of the balance of nature, this causes no problem. But on plantations, where they are competing with humans for food, they can become a serious pest.

An ant can carry a piece of leaf more than twice its size

Ants returning to collect more leaves

HONEYPOT ANTS
In semidesert areas all over the world different species of ant have independently evolved the same remarkable way of staying alive in the dry season. During the rains, the ants feed some of their workers with water and nectar. These workers store the extra food in their crop, and the front part of their abdomen swells. They cannot move around but hang upside down in the nest as living larders, for use by the rest of the colony during the long, flowerless dry season.

STITCHED UP
Some ants in tropical areas from Africa to Australia build nests in trees by "sewing" together groups of large leaves. A row of worker ants pulls two leaves together.
When the edges are close, more workers, each holding a live ant larva in their jaws, sew the leaves together using strands of silk produced by the larva's salivary glands. The finished nest (right) is a ball of leaves. If the nest is disturbed, the thousands of weaver ants give a noisy warning by tapping on the leaves from within.
When these ants bite, they squirt formic acid into the wound, making it doubly painful.

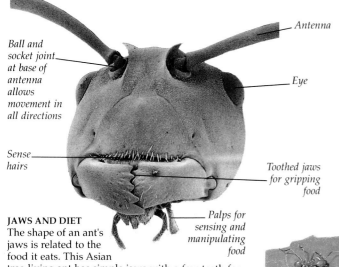

Antenna

Ball and socket joint at base of antenna allows movement in all directions

Eye

Sense hairs

Toothed jaws for gripping food

JAWS AND DIET
The shape of an ant's jaws is related to the food it eats. This Asian tree-living ant has simple jaws with a few teeth for feeding on soft insects and honeydew (p. 21). Most ants are predators with long, slender, pointed jaws; but some species have become plant-feeders. Harvester ants have broad-tipped crushing jaws without teeth for feeding on grass seeds.

Palps for sensing and manipulating food

Parasol ants cut out pieces of leaves, which they then carry back to the nest

Ant

Two ants cut out a large piece of leaf with their powerful cutting jaws

A LEAFY TRAIL
The trails of small green leaves are often very clear during the day where they cross footpaths on the route back to the nest. Outward-bound workers can be seen stopping and encouraging their laden colleagues. Sometimes a "parasol" is dropped; then several ants rush forward and hoist it into the air to be carried home by one of them.

The "parasols" of these leaf-cutting ants are pieces of leaves and flowers

FAIR-WEATHER WORKERS
Parasol ants do not collect leaves when it is raining, and if a heavy shower occurs while they are out cutting, the leaves are usually dropped outside the nest. Perhaps wet leaves would upset the delicate balance inside the fungus gardens and endanger the colony's food supply.

Honeybees and hives

PEOPLE HAVE COLLECTED HONEY from the nests of bees for many centuries. The oldest record is a cave painting in Spain, nearly 9,000 years old, which shows a figure apparently taking honey from a nest on a cliff – a practice still followed today in some parts of the world. Egyptian tomb decorations indicate that humans were keeping bees, not just robbing wild nests, 2,500 years ago, and methods changed little until recently. Only during the last hundred years have efforts been made to breed docile bees that produce a lot of honey. In a modern domestic hive, there are three types of honeybee (*Apis mellifera*): one queen, a fertile, mated female who lays all the eggs – sometimes over 1,000 a day; a few hundred males called drones, whose only function is to fertilize new queens; and up to 60,000 sterile female workers, who do all the work in the hive.

BUSY BEES
Straw "bee skeps," like this one drawn 400 years ago, changed little for thousands of years. Inside, the bees built their own combs on a supporting stick.

SWARMING
A bee colony produces a few new queens each year. Just before the first queen emerges from her pupa, the old queen and about half the workers fly away as a swarm. Swarming bees are often docile, and this engraving shows a swarm being gathered into a straw skep. The first new queen to emerge in the old nest normally kills her rivals so she can reign supreme.

LOWER FRAME FROM HIVE
On the lower frames of a hive honey and pollen are stored in the upper cells, and the brood is reared in the lower cells, as shown here. When a bee finds a source of nectar, it flies back to the hive and performs a curious "dance" on the comb. This tells other bees how close the food is and where it lies in relation to the position of the sun. Bees foraging in open country make a "beeline" between the hive and the food source that is as busy as a highway.

Large drone cells

Outside cover

Inside cover

Shallow super

Queen excluder – a grid with slots too narrow to let the queen through into the upper combs

MODERN HIVES
The modern Langstroth hive was invented in 1851 in Philadelphia. The bees are provided with combs in removable frames; a lower set for the brood chamber, and an upper set ("shallow super") for storing nectar and pollen. The queen is prevented from laying eggs in the upper combs by the "queen excluder."

Brood chamber

Bottom board with hive entrance

Cell walls are made of wax, which the workers produce in flakes from glands between the joints of their abdomens

Honey

Honeycomb

HONEY
Combs from a hive, with the cells full of honey, are often sold as a delicacy.

BUMBLEBEES
Bumblebees, big hairy bees of the northern temperate region, are very important for pollinating some crops. They usually nest in the burrows of small mammals and construct a few irregularly shaped cells.

BEE BONNET
Swarming bees can be very docile. This swarm has been encouraged to sit on a man's head. He probably first placed the queen on his head in a small cage, so that the workers would gather around her.

White wax-capped cells contain honey for feeding developing grubs – and the beekeeper

Yellow-capped cells at top of comb contain pollen stores

Young C-shaped grubs at bottom of wax cells

Eggs

Young grub

Mature grub

Pupa

LIFE STAGES
Bees undergo complete metamorphosis (pp. 24–25). As the eggs develop into grubs and then pupae, they are fed and looked after by young workers. Older workers look for food outside the hive.

Older workers bring back pollen to hive, where it is stored in cells to feed the developing grubs

The yellow silk-capped cells in the lower half of the frame contain pupae

Newly hatched grubs are fed first on royal jelly, a special saliva produced by the workers, then on honey

Helpful and harmful

INSECTS ARE ESSENTIAL to the well-being of the living world. Bees, flies, and butterflies help pollinate our crops and so insure that fruit and seeds are produced. Wasps and ladybirds destroy the caterpillars and aphids that attack our plants. Beetles and flies clean up animal dung and the rotting bodies of dead plants and animals, recycling the nutrients for use by new generations of plants. Many animals rely on insects for food, and in many parts of the world people traditionally eat fat, juicy caterpillars and grubs. Bees provide us with honey and beeswax; moth caterpillars produce silk; and food coloring is made from the crushed bodies of certain bugs. But people often notice insects only when they become a nuisance or a threat. Many insects transmit diseases to people, animals, and plants and every year they are responsible for the destruction of between 10 and 15 percent of the world's food.

Harvesting cochineal insects

DYES AND MANNA
Cochineal is a red food coloring extracted from the crushed bodies of scale insects (*Dactylopius coccus*). Originally from Mexico, these tiny bugs (p. 36) and the opuntia cacti on which they feed are now cultivated in other hot, dry countries. The biblical manna that fed the children of Israel was probably derived from similar bugs on tamarisk trees.

Cochineal coloring

POISON DARTS
The pupae of this African leaf beetle (*Polyclada bohemani*) contain a remarkably powerful poison. South African bushmen used to use this poison on their arrows when hunting.

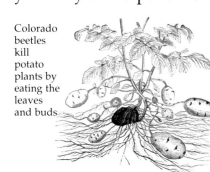

Colorado beetles kill potato plants by eating the leaves and buds

COLORADO BEETLE
The Colorado beetle (*Leptinotarsa decemlineata*) used to feed harmlessly on leaves in the Rocky Mountains. But when settlers introduced potatoes there in about 1850, the beetle developed a taste for this new food and swept eastward across America devastating potato patch after potato patch. In the days before insecticides it was a serious pest because it eats the leaves and buds, and stops the plant's growth.

PERIODIC PEST
This longhorn beetle (*Hoplocerambyx spinocorrus*) usually attacks dead and dying sal trees in India. The grubs drill large tunnels in the timber. But sometimes the population increases rapidly, and living trees are attacked. The worst outbreak resulted in damage to one million trees, with serious financial loss to the foresters.

Death watch beetles can reduce structural timbers to little more than a skeleton

CIGARETTE BEETLES
Smoking is harmful to your health. But cigarette beetle grubs (*Lasioderma serricorne*) do not read the health warnings (the adults do not feed at all). Sixty years ago, one way to get the beetles out of a horsehair-stuffed settee was to soak the furniture in gasoline. This too is harmful to your health, particularly if you are smoking at the time.

DEATH WATCH
Death watch beetles (*Xestobium rufovillosum*) can be serious pests of timber in houses. In spring, the noise of the adults tapping the front of their heads against the wood as a mating call has been linked superstitiously with approaching death. But the most likely disaster it heralds is the house falling down.

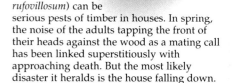

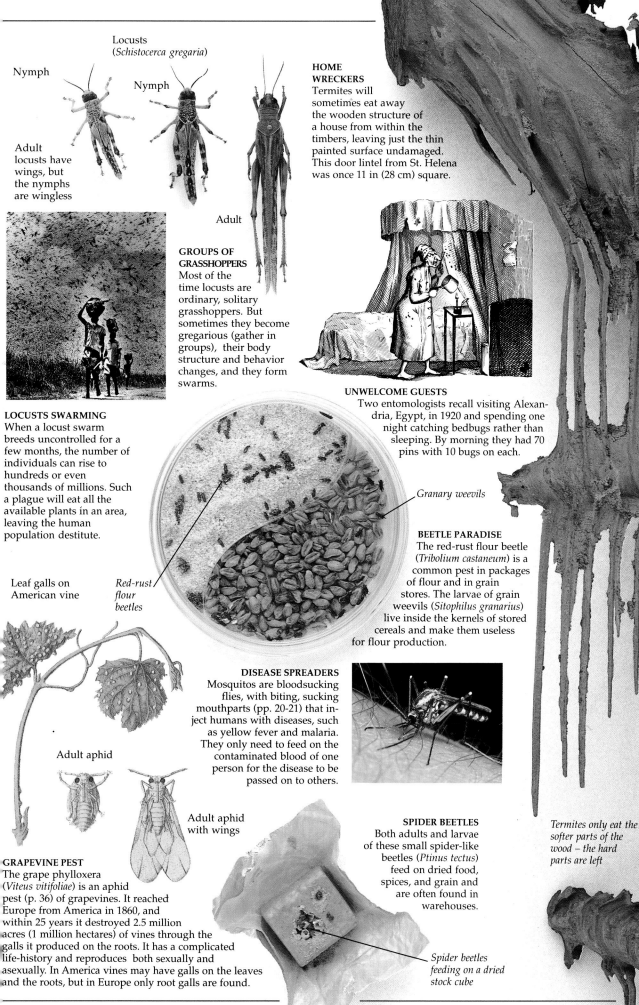

Locusts
(Schistocerca gregaria)

Nymph

Nymph

Adult
locusts have
wings, but
the nymphs
are wingless

Adult

GROUPS OF GRASSHOPPERS
Most of the
time locusts are
ordinary, solitary
grasshoppers. But
sometimes they become
gregarious (gather in
groups), their body
structure and behavior
changes, and they form
swarms.

HOME WRECKERS
Termites will
sometimes eat away
the wooden structure of
a house from within the
timbers, leaving just the thin
painted surface undamaged.
This door lintel from St. Helena
was once 11 in (28 cm) square.

UNWELCOME GUESTS
Two entomologists recall visiting Alexan-
dria, Egypt, in 1920 and spending one
night catching bedbugs rather than
sleeping. By morning they had 70
pins with 10 bugs on each.

LOCUSTS SWARMING
When a locust swarm
breeds uncontrolled for a
few months, the number of
individuals can rise to
hundreds or even
thousands of millions. Such
a plague will eat all the
available plants in an area,
leaving the human
population destitute.

Granary weevils

BEETLE PARADISE
The red-rust flour beetle
(*Tribolium castaneum*) is a
common pest in packages
of flour and in grain
stores. The larvae of grain
weevils (*Sitophilus granarius*)
live inside the kernels of stored
cereals and make them useless
for flour production.

Leaf galls on
American vine

*Red-rust
flour
beetles*

DISEASE SPREADERS
Mosquitos are bloodsucking
flies, with biting, sucking
mouthparts (pp. 20-21) that inject humans with diseases, such
as yellow fever and malaria.
They only need to feed on the
contaminated blood of one
person for the disease to be
passed on to others.

Adult aphid

Adult aphid
with wings

SPIDER BEETLES
Both adults and larvae
of these small spider-like
beetles (*Ptinus tectus*)
feed on dried food,
spices, and grain
and are often found in
warehouses.

*Termites only eat the
softer parts of the
wood – the hard
parts are left*

GRAPEVINE PEST
The grape phylloxera
(*Viteus vitifoliae*) is an aphid
pest (p. 36) of grapevines. It reached
Europe from America in 1860, and
within 25 years it destroyed 2.5 million
acres (1 million hectares) of vines through the
galls it produced on the roots. It has a complicated
life-history and reproduces both sexually and
asexually. In America vines may have galls on the leaves
and the roots, but in Europe only root galls are found.

*Spider beetles
feeding on a dried
stock cube*

Looking at insects

MORE THAN THREE CENTURIES of studying and collecting insects have made it possible to recognize most of the insect species in Europe. But it is still impossible to guess how many different species live in parts of North America and less well-explored tropical countries. Today, insect collecting should be concerned with examining the ways in which insects help maintain the balance of nature. How important are they for pollinating flowers and trees? Which insects are needed to decompose wood and dead leaves and produce nutrients for new plants? How many insects are needed to feed other animals? But looking at insects can also be fun. At its simplest, all it requires is patience and good eyesight – possibly helped by a magnifying glass and a camera. Just observing how these fascinating creatures live is an important way of learning how the natural world works.

INSECT INTEREST
In the 19th century, interest in natural history became fashionable, and private collections of insects, plants, and minerals were common. This engraving is of an elaborate glass tank called a vivarium, in which the life histories of living insects could be observed.

JEAN FABRE (1823-1915)
The French naturalist Jean Henri Fabre wrote many popular books about the lives of insects.

Chloroform bottle and top

Carrying ring

Nozzle

Airtight top

CHLOROFORM BOTTLE
One method of killing freshly caught specimens was to shake a few drops of chloroform from the pointed nozzle of a brass container such as this.

IVORY HANDLES
Before the invention of plastic, small pieces of apparatus were made from fine materials such as brass and ivory. This mounted lens, on which specimens can be fixed at an adjustable height, was used for many years by the English insect scientist Edward Meyrick (1854-1938).

Ivory-handled pin

Specimen fixed in front of lens for examination

Dustproof leather case

Folding brass lens

HAND LENS
Magnifying glasses were once common, from large low-powered lenses to small, expensive ones which magnified ten or even 25 times and often folded up to fit in a pocket.

Small high-power lens

Cork

Insects pinned into cork

COLLECTING TIN
Insect collectors and entomologists pinned the fragile specimens they caught outdoors in special cork-lined tins, like this one, which was made in France.

FIELD DIARY
The most devoted students kept detailed notebooks of their observations on live insects. The diaries of the English entomologist Charles Dubois (1656-1740) include notes of the insects he saw, sometimes with drawings and comments on their habits and appearance.

Scissor-like handles

SCISSOR NET
To catch an insect, the two flat sheets of muslin of this old-fashioned scissor net could be snapped shut.

Square tips for holding pins

Fine points for tiny insects

Opticians' forceps

Finely woven cotton muslin prevents the captured insect from escaping

Metal needle holder

Tweezers

TOOLS
Opticians' forceps with fine points are useful for picking up tiny specimens. In contrast, tweezers with square tips are used for holding pins. Needles of differing sizes can be mounted into metal handles, so that single legs or antennae can be positioned.

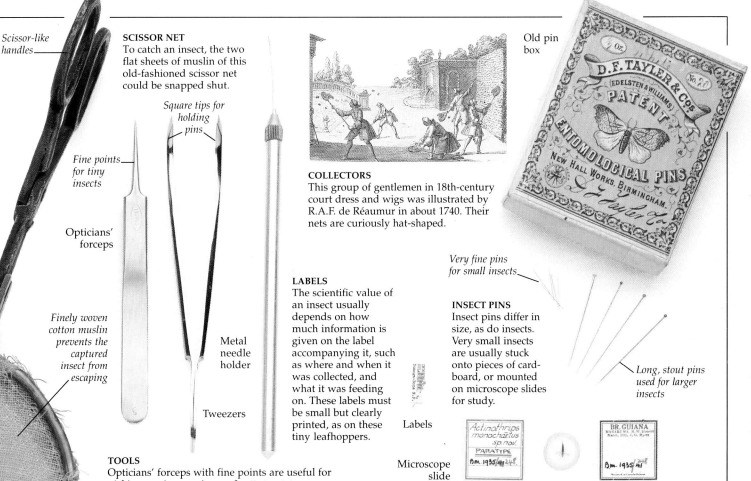

COLLECTORS
This group of gentlemen in 18th-century court dress and wigs was illustrated by R.A.F. de Réaumur in about 1740. Their nets are curiously hat-shaped.

Old pin box

LABELS
The scientific value of an insect usually depends on how much information is given on the label accompanying it, such as where and when it was collected, and what it was feeding on. These labels must be small but clearly printed, as on these tiny leafhoppers.

Labels

Microscope slide

Very fine pins for small insects

INSECT PINS
Insect pins differ in size, as do insects. Very small insects are usually stuck onto pieces of cardboard, or mounted on microscope slides for study.

Long, stout pins used for larger insects

Actinothrips
monochaetus
sp. nov.
PARATYPE
Bm. 1935/248.

BR. GUIANA
Bm. 1935/248

SMALL INSECTS
Many insect species are less than 0.04 in (1 mm) long – too small to be pinned. They are usually collected into alcohol, stored in small glass vials, and studied under a microscope on glass slides, in watch glasses, or in small glass dishes.

Glass dish containing alcohol

Base of box is lined with white plastic foam

MODERN PLASTIC COLLECTION BOX
The advantage of plastic is that it is not as heavy as metal, and collections can be seen without removing the lid. This is a typical collection of small moths attracted to a light trap at night.

MODERN TRAPS
The Malaise trap catches large numbers of flying insects. When they fly into the central wall, most crawl upward into the bottle at the top – although some drop to the ground and crawl away.

Extinction
In recent years, radical changes in land use have reduced forests and other natural habitats all over the world. As a result many insect species are vanishing – some of them becoming extinct before they have ever been discovered. The St. Helena earwig is a very large insect that used to live only on the island of St. Helena in the middle of the South Atlantic Ocean. It has not been seen alive for many years and is probably now extinct.

Extinct St. Helena earwig

Index

Acknowledgments

The author would like to thank:
his many colleagues at the Natural History Museum who helped with this project, particularly Sharon Shute, Judith Marshall, Bill Dolling, George Else, David Carter, Nigel Fergusson, John Chainey, Steve Brooks, Nigel Wyatt, Philip Ackery, Peter Broomfield, Bill Sands, Barry Bolton, Mick Day, Dick Vane-Wright.
Dorling Kindersley would like to thank:
London Zoo for help with photography of ants on pp. 56-57.
Syon House for supplying specimens.
Julie Harvey at the Natural History Museum.
Stephen Oliver for close-up shots on pp. 9, 45, 58.
Dave King for special photography on pp. 56-57.

Picture credits

t = top b = bottom m = middle l = left
r = right

Aldus Archive: 61bl
Angel, Heather/Biofotos: 7br; 10m; 11tr
Biophoto Associates: 36ml; 41br
Borrell, B./Frank Lane Picture Agency: 56tr
Bunn, D.S.: 50tl
Burton, Jane/Bruce Coleman: 31b; 34mr; 36tl; 39br
Cane, W./Natural Science Photos: 32m; 61bm
Clarke, Dave: 23tm; 47b
Clyne, Densey/OSF: 57tl; 57tm; 57tr
Cooke, J.A.L./OSF: 12tl
Couch, C./Natural History Museum: 15br
Craven, Philip/Robert Harding Picture Library: 7t

Dalton, Stephen/NHPA: 37ml
David, Jules/Fine Art Photos: 38tr
Mary Evans Picture Library: 61tm
Fogden, Michael/OSF: 10ml
Goodman, Jeff/NHPA: 9ml
Holford, Michael: 15mr
Hosking, E. & D.:39tm
James, E.A./NHPA: 46br
King, Ken/Planet Earth: 57m
Kobal Collection: 40tl
Krasemann, S./NHPA: 47tr
Lofthouse, Barbara: 25tr
Mackenzie, M.A./Robert Harding Picture Library: 37br
National Film Archive: 32tl
Natural History Museum: 12tr; 14bl
Overcash, David/Bruce Coleman: 15bl
Oxford Scientific Films: 20tl
Packwood, Richard/OSF: 56tr
Pitkin, Brian/Natural History Museum: 42m

Popperfoto: 61tl
Robert Harding Picture Library: 30tl
Rutherford, Gary/Bruce Coleman: 7bm
Sands, Bill: 55m
Shay, A./OSF: 20bm
Springate, N.D./Natural History Museum: 63bm
Taylor, Kim/Bruce Coleman: 21tl; 31b
Taylor, Kim: 33m
Vane-Wright, Dick/Natural History Museum: 16br
Ward, P.H. & S.L./Natural Science Photos: 44mr
Williams, C./Natural Science Photos: 36ml

Illustrations by: John Woodcock: pp. 10, 41, 55; Nick Hall: pp. 13, 15

Picture research by: Kathy Lockley